COMPROMISE

(Horses and Souls
Book Two)

Anna Rashbrook

WITH THANKS
Dave, my husband for bearing with my
determined sitting at the PC.

To Jenny, my first reader, who always puts me
right!
Ann Trump Preier for her fantastic editing.

My beta readers, Stephanie, Amanda, Tanya and
Chris

To Kevin.J.Wilson, who read and re-read for me,
beyond the call of duty!

Especial thanks to the photographer, Deske
Wijers, who has allowed me to us the image of her
stallion, Dennis for th cover!

ALSO BY ANNA RASHBROOK

The Horses and Souls Series

Challenger
Compromise
Chaos
Christmas
Castles in the Air
Collection
Conclusion

The God, horses, and love Memoirs

Was it all about horses?
Finding
Horses and Heartbreak

Travel

Dear Boot
Wish You Were Here - Holiday Memoirs; An anthology of travel stories (The Travel Stories Series)
The Travel stories Collection (The Travel Stori*es Series)*

Supernatural Thriller

Tom

Blogs

'So Where's the Snow?'
https://annarashbrook.wordpress.com

Anna's Horse Books
https://annarashbrook.wordpress.com

CONTENTS

ONE

Mollie opened the back door to let the dogs out into the garden and smelt the new morning. Somewhere a blackbird was singing despite their snufflings and barging about. Dew lay thickly on the grass and the faint smell of the peonies was in the air. Another day, another repetition of lessons, mucking out, cleaning tack, walking dogs. Just where was life going? There seemed to be no direction any more. Both dogs came scurrying in, ready for the next stage of their wonderfully ordered routine, which included toast and trying to get the cat's bowl down off the dresser before he had finished. All too soon, it was time to go to the yard, and once again the car wouldn't start. Ratty, the black collie cross, sat patiently on the front seat as the flooded petrol leaked away, with Mollie absentmindedly stroking her. Once upon a time, she would have prayed about it, but she knew now it wouldn't work. Mutantmutt jealously put her head on Mollie's shoulder, leaving it covered in brown, white, and grey hairs. The third turn and the engine chugged, sprang into life and they were on their way.

She was still first at the stable-yard, savouring the moment of the twenty eager heads appearing over box doors with low whickers of complete cupboard love in aid of getting their breakfast earlier than expected. The three-sided yard looked like a picture book with the green painted stable doors and red brick. The recent extension had been so carefully done that you wouldn't know they weren't the original Victorian Hazeley stables. Despite their old look, they were one of the best stables in the area, run by Liz of the iron hand, with Mollie as yard manager.

The others always missed this reception as the heads were firmly in mangers when they arrived. Swiftly stepping over the yard dogs, Mollie went to the feed room and collected the premade feed bowls. There was something to be said for an orderly regime. Five minutes in the evening was worth half an hour in the morning, and the new stables had feeders in the doors, so there was no barging in and out of boxes as the horses tried to snatch a quick mouthful. Munching noises filled the yard, and Mollie took the time to look at the horses feeding. All were eating well, no rugs slipped, and hay nets all emptied; that was good. Another routine day; even Keith the stallion was feeding as if he never thought of anything else.

The sound of tyres heralded the arrival of the others – car sharing from the town as usual. Slamming of doors and barking; Mollie's dogs could never get used to the two tschitzus that belonged to Tina. Well, at least this was a job where dogs were welcome. The three girls went straight to the tack room for a brew without looking at the horses. They knew Mollie would have already fed the horses and the kettle was soon on.

'How did the Pub quiz go last night?' Mollie

asked.

'We won –YAY!' replied Tina with a smirk.

'Great, I suppose it's the White Horse Inn for the finals then?' Tina nodded, and the conversation foundered. As usual, there wasn't quite enough water for Mollie's coffee, but she was used to it. As usual, she then said, 'I'd better do the feed bowls' and left them to it. Shutting the door, she heard the conversation begin with giggles, and it hurt as much as usual. She looked down and saw she had her purple jodhs on again with the lime green t-shirt. Would she ever learn? At least this time they hadn't laughed and then shaken their heads in disbelief at her fashion sense before saying so. Working alone with Tina or Heather or Sue was no problem. It was just them as a group, which made her feel fat and awkward, forever the outsider. Maybe it didn't help them all living in the town and being a generation younger than herself. She should be used to it by now.

Feed bowls rinsed, it was time for mucking out. Mollie went to collect her wheelbarrow; being first, she got the best tools this way. Liz was just coming out of the flat. Maybe today she might get a hack with the kids, and not more lunging... To her surprise, Liz was coming straight in her direction and smiling. Late middle-aged with iron-grey hair, she ran the yard with orderly precision. This Mollie appreciated, but not the withholding of information such as the daily ride order. Maybe it was a control thing, yet Liz would never let the daybook out of her locked office. She was still smiling; this was not good at this time of the day. Usually, she went straight to the office and didn't emerge till the yard was being swept, as if there was the most enormous amount of paperwork to be done.

'Morning, Mollie, could you just pop into the office with me?' Mollie felt sick and sicker as Liz twiddled with the locks.

'Do sit down.' Even worse, it must be the sack.

'Now, as you know, there's been some conversation about the future of Keith.' Mollie didn't, but this was a better turn than expected.

'Last summer was a nightmare with the mares arriving just as the school hols were starting, let alone with the lack of boxes. So, we've decided to put him free range!' Liz smiled conspiratorially. 'Most of the owners, as you know, left their mares here for three weeks or more, especially when they had to be collected at the weekends. We're going to put Keith up onto the hill, grazing at Chris Brown's place and run the mares with him. He's an experienced stallion man, having had his own stud in the past.'

'What has this to do with me?' thought Mollie, and then the penny dropped. She was the only one who could drive the box.

'Now we will need someone to go at least once a week with the mares, as most boxes won't get up that steep lane. You'll have to liaise with Chris so that you can do trips loaded both ways. He's happy to remove any shoes, too.' Mollie's heart sank to her boots — all that driving and time away from the yard.

'I'm sorry, this will fall onto your shoulders, but we will try to get Tina's licence sorted out,' Liz was continuing. 'I will pay you for all your time away from the yard as if you were here.'

I should think so, too.

'And overtime if you get held up. You may take the dogs, of course.' Crumbs, getting overtime was like blood and stone usually. The whole arrangement didn't seem right to her, but what was she to say?

Liz was still smiling, and Mollie realised that for once she hadn't been sure of her reception; she may even have expected Mollie to refuse. For a moment the opportunity was there, and yet again, with her slow thinking, she'd missed the opportunity and it was gone, for Liz was standing as if to usher her out.

'I'm, yes, well fine, but I may need some help unloading.'

'Chris will do that; he's met Keith.'

Mollie was grasping for straws. 'What about my regular clients? I'd hate to lose that continuity that we've tried to build up (one of Liz's own mottoes).'

'I'm sure we'll be able to work around that. The other girls can always load and get everything ready, and I'll keep an eye on the book.' Liz patted its closed cover, smiling yet again. 'Oh no, she's lying,' thought Mollie, but couldn't see any way to escape or run away from the abyss opening before her. The others would never lift a finger to help her. The one thing that kept her going was that bunch of cheeky kids who came regularly to ride after school. Oh, maybe it wouldn't be so bad; she always reacted negatively to new things. Time away from the yard might be good; the dogs would enjoy the walk if she had to go and catch the mares. If she could just hang onto her 4:30 slot... She gave Liz a small smile and went to muck out.

Six thirty had the dogs investigating the back garden in case there'd been any intruders during the day, while Mollie sat on the back step in the sunshine, nursing a beer before she made any decisions about food. All the events of the day were going around and around in her head; she was imposing all the answers and snap humour she should have made. How she had such a struggle with her 3:30 lesson, which hadn't gone well until she found out that the kid had been in bed all week with a cold and the mother had pushed her to come. Parents!

Eventually, even Mollie saw it was futile and it was best to put things to bed. She drained her beer and went to see what enticing ready meal she would devour tonight, well at least the dogs would. Blinking as she went into the dark room, she heard the phone ringing in the hall and stumbled over dogs, piles of books and the old carpet in her haste. She got there in time and was regaled with a deeply chocolate male voice asking for her in person. 'If only,' she thought!

'It's James Whitaker, just confirming that I'll be arriving tomorrow morning at about 12 at Rose cottage and I hope all the paperwork has reached you!'

Her heart sank. She'd forgotten the new tenant next door. Why wouldn't her parents just sell the place, not keep going on about keeping it for her to knock through when she needed to expand the house…

'Yes, everything's in order. Your boxes have been put in the garage. I'm right next door, so please just come and knock when you arrive. Are you okay with dogs?'

'Why, are they moving in, too?'

'No, just I have two and they may meet you first!'

'No problem!'

He rang off and Mollie, not for the first time, wondered if she was in the right job. She loved horses but working day in and out with them was robbing her of her joy in them, whereas she could very efficiently organise cleaners and lettings for next door if her parents would just let her. She could make a real going concern with lettings for riders and horsey holidaymakers. Still, tomorrow was the start of her weekend off. She would for a short while be a horse-free zone, and after whatshisname had arrived, she would go shopping. Yes, Primark was calling.

Promptly at midday, the dogs outside began to bark, and Mollie had her hand on the door handle before the bell rang. She'd found some reasonable jeans and a fairly ironed looking t-shirt ready for her trip to the town and was impatient to get going. She had the keys in her hand. What she hadn't expected was the discrepancy between the voice and the person. For what stood on the doorstep was thin enough to be an escapee from Belsen and tall enough to regularly have concussion from the cottage beams. Another charity case of her parents; no doubt reduced rates again. It would be nice to make a decent profit on the cottage one day. All this flashed through her head as she prepared herself to smile. Of course, at this moment Mutantmutt launched herself at her favourite part of the new love of her life, which normally was usually the stomach, but this time was the back of his legs. She propelled James through the front door and onto Mollie, who fell backwards, with James landing on her. Momentarily winded and speechless, Mollie could do nothing but stare into a startlingly deep brown pair of eyes. Ratty had come to join in and now was doing her growling at strangers' routine with lips bared.

'You mentioned dogs, didn't you?' James grimaced and levered himself off. Mollie was still trying to breathe and couldn't answer. He took her hands and hauled her to her feet as she gasped for breath.

'I'm ssooo sorry,' was all she could finally master. 'Ratty, Mutt, basket!' The two knew it was a step too far and sloped off, nobody loved them anymore. James was smiling, smiling too much. Oh boy, she'd really blown it. She was stumped for words and so just gave him the keys.

'I really am sorry. That's never happened before. I'll keep them under control.'

'They don't do that double act every time visitors arrive?'

'No, thank heavens.'

James' good humour was defusing the situation.

'Let me show you around.' Mollie led the way through the gap in the hedge and opened the front door of the adjoining cottage. James followed, and she saw him automatically ducking behind her. Maybe his height wouldn't be such a problem; he was trained. Mollie went into her automatic explanation of the water, heating, bin bags and so on, while James nodded with a pleasant expression on his face and took in what she was saying. Model tenant and landlady stuff, so she was out and shutting the door in ten minutes. Then the embarrassment kicked in. She couldn't get in the car quick enough and escape.

James sat wearily on the sofa and shut his eyes; all that smiling was just too exhausting. What he would have given to have kicked that bleeding dog in the nads, down the garden and onto the road! Still, when you've got a really cheap deal on a let with some peace and quiet to write, what can you do? At that very moment, the dogs, now shut in, began to bark. He leapt up and banged on the adjoining wall, which, to his relief, worked. Once he had everything set up, he could wear his headphones as he wrote and that would shut the noise out. He saw some of Mollie's jodhs drying on the line and was reminded that was the first time he'd been astride a woman for months, and she was nicely rounded!

He steadily fetched his boxes out of the garage and unpacked. Laptop worked, the internet functioned – you never could be sure in the back of the woods. He found his favourite Cezanne and put that over the fireplace, removing the dark hunting print. In the kitchen, he found no food, just a few tired teabags. A quick trip onto Tesco's website soon sorted that out. He was darned if he was doing the chatting in the village shop with the locals; he'd done his duty on that for years. Medicines and bath stuff into the small bathroom – no shaving for him for a while. He put his little tin by the laptop ready for later. He slung his clothes into drawers, jamming them shut ignoring the previous ironings. He'd just grabbed a selection when he'd left. The thick quilt on the bed was appealing – a quick snooze, until the goodies arrived, then down to work. He settled himself contentedly under it, not even kicking his shoes off.

'Keith is a completely stupid name for a horse,' thought Chris as the stallion reversed himself out of the box. Especially as he was such a good specimen. A real Welsh Cob, true palomino, quarters to eat your dinner off and a huge firm crest covered by a flowing white mane. No, he wasn't going to think blonde. The horse raised his head and neighed with the imperious voice of his sex, his body quivering with excitement. Tail held like a banner, he then proceeded to try to cavort around the yard. Chris could see it, he was yelling for where the girls were, or if anyone wanted a fight. With an adept yank of the rope, he brought the horse's head down and the rest of him to a halt. He stroked the quivering nose. 'All in good time, mate!'

Chris led him through the stable yard, and out towards the field where he would spend a few nights settling in with his own two mares until the visitors started arriving. Releasing the rope, he expected Keith to take off to his mares who were standing under the tree, completely gobsmacked at the arrival of their Adonis. But no, Keith for some reason was convinced that the action was all in the yard and he paced backwards and forwards by the gate, yelling his head off. His pace picked up and finally, he turned and swung in an arc as if to jump the gate. Chris strode to the gate and waved his arms and yelled, diverting the stallion's attention at the last minute, sending him swerving up the field where he finally saw the mares and the penny dropped. Keith cavorted off to check out the action. Relieved, Chris leant on the gate to make sure all went to order. Mollie joined him at the gate, having swept out the trailer and stowed some bits and pieces.

'Well, I suppose that was par for the course for him. I know he's a splendid Welsh, but I can't help but think he's, well, just a little blonde...' Mollie remarked.

Chris turned to her, surprised. 'Most women are soppy over stallions and their lovely manes! But I suppose when all you can think about is sex, it does stunt the brain cells!' He laughed, and they both blushed furiously.

'Coming in for a cup of tea?' he babbled. Darn, he really didn't have time for this...

'That would be great, can I let the dogs out?'

'Sure, I'll let Rex loose; he's not at all aggressive when he's off the chain.' They walked back to the yard and the shaggy old Alsatian was released to greet some new faces with apparent delight. Mollie followed Chris indoors. She'd known him for a few years through the stables and meeting at shows. It seemed the usually quiet man was more talkative on his home territory. The corridor was lined with hooks laden with old jackets, with hats, boots and boxes on the floor. The kitchen was warm through the aga's glow. It was painted in pale cream with the ever-present huge table littered with paperwork. On the walls hung some tack and rosettes from shows. A home from home, Mollie felt. She could never really do the horsey thing at her cottage because the parents still owned it and kept an eye on her through Jane, her cleaner.

Steaming cups in hand, they both sat at the table for a few minutes in silence, both trying to think of what to say.

'I suppose Liz sprung this on you in her usual manner?' Chris finally asked.

Mollie nodded.' I just hope it doesn't keep me away from the yard too much.'

'I told her I could come and collect anytime after hay is done.'

'Yeah, but you'd charge more!'

They smiled, finding their mutual company away from the yard and people suddenly easier than expected, but, nevertheless, they drank their tea swiftly.

'Have you any idea when the first mare's arriving?'

'Your guess is as good as mine; I'm afraid Liz only gives out the minimum of information. I expect she'll ring you the night before. I still can't understand her decision fully. It seems so risky with the mares. There could be injuries and the covering dates might not be right.' Chris didn't comment. Mollie glanced awkwardly at her watch. 'Now I must head back. I need to time these journeys for future trips.' They both went out through the cool dairy this time, Mollie admiring the old equipment that was being used. 'Are you still making cheese then?'

'Just a bit. After Mum and Dad died, there just hasn't been the time; I've let things slide a bit. I'll have to get some paid help this summer, I think.'

'There's definitely a market for it here with the increase in holiday people; we have so many more riders now in the summer.'

'Well, I'll see. I just hope that dumb blonde doesn't complicate things too much!' They both laughed and looked up at the paddock where nature was taking its due course. Mollie collected the dogs, who were all lying together in the sun, and drove away. 'Nice bloke,' she thought. Funny how you never really get to know people when you're always rushing around. Then an image of Chris just now came to mind – he'd been wearing an almost peacock blue pair of dungarees which were too short for him, with an orange spotted t-shirt and the standard farmer's sun hat in green. Not just me with no colour sense!

TWO

Mollie's life was complicated enough, and now Mutantmutt had made it even better by coming into season. And being her, it was full blast from day one, with drips on the floor and outrageous behaviour between her and Ratty, often ending in a fight. Mollie not only had to keep Mutantmutt in Purdah, but she also had to keep her separate from Ratty. She didn't dare take her to the yard, so Mutantmutt stayed home with treats and plenty to eat and drink, hopefully, in the most soundly insulated room in the house, the kitchen. Mollie felt a heel the first day she left her, even momentarily weakening and thinking of just leaving her in the car or a stable, but that had led to a lot of damaged paint both in and out last time. Mollie cursed herself for not remembering to take Mutantmutt on the trip to that nice man in the white coat with the operating table.

James had been really enjoying the peace and quiet. He'd written 50,000 words in the couple of weeks he'd been closeted, and this time the plot really was shaping nicely. He leant away from the table and the laptop, stretching till his knuckles cracked. No nagging, no social life, no shopping… ah, he needed to call Tesco's. As he rummaged in the cupboard to find his tin, he became aware of the most peculiar noise, something like singing, or a moan, or a long sigh, and it warbled. He walked around the flat trying to pinpoint the noise, some rooms louder, worst in his sitting room. It droned on and on and on. He banged on the wall, but it continued. Perhaps it was a disc or a faulty appliance in Mollie's kitchen. He'd heard her leave, so he was stuck with this noise all day long. He felt himself tensing up. He had to have quiet, or he just couldn't write. He'd lose the flow. He began to panic, his breathing quickening. Then he remembered his relaxation exercises and positive thinking and sat down to try and calm. It didn't work, because now something was scratching at the wall. His fury arose, and he picked up a chair and slung it at the wall. It hit and fell to bits leaving a dent. Next door was filled with barking. It was one of those flaming dogs. He hammered on the wall, dust flew, and the barking stopped. James relaxed and felt himself begin to unwind. 'Calm down,' he thought. 'It's ok, back to the plot', but then the moaning began again…

Now he wanted to weep. He'd never be able to write again. Then he remembered his headphones and the iPod; the white noise would drown everything out. Headphones, no iPod. He began to pace again; then he saw the elderly music centre under the TV, but not so elderly that his headphones didn't fit. Salvation! He soon tuned it into a classical station and, put at a low level, that was enough to drown the low-level frequency moaning. Order for food made, James began on a brilliant new stream of consciousness that would engulf his narrative in new depth and meaning. He worked for the rest of the day in relative contentment.

Mollie managed to get away quickly from work at lunchtime, and as she drove home, she prayed that Mutantmutt's bladder had held for the morning. As she parked, she became aware of the most deafening music she had ever heard. Full blast classical that seemed to shake the plaster out of the windows of next door. She'd forgotten to tell James about the enormous speakers hidden behind the settee. Banging on the door got no response. She could see James bent over his laptop, wearing headphones oblivious to the surrounding noise. He couldn't have known about switching the system over to headphones only; he was set on both. Waving and blocking the light had no effect either. Mollie had to rescue Mutant, so gave up and went indoors. If anything, it was louder inside. Mutantmutt was fine and went out into the garden. Then Mollie had an inspiration. She found James's mobile number and sent him a text. Two minutes later, the music stopped. The door front banged, and he barged in.

James towered over her. 'If you would keep your stupid dogs under control, there wouldn't be a problem! I lost hours of work with the flaming noise and now it seems I'm at fault for the loud music!' He glowered down at her.

'Look, I'm sorry, I have to leave her at home because she's in season.'

'Not my flaming problem. I pay good money for this peace; I will not have it ruined! I'll complain to your parents and if that doesn't work, I'll call the police!'

'Thank heavens her parents were abroad!' His voice got louder and louder and he seemed to grow taller. Mollie shrank back away from him. 'I'm sorry, but I don't have many options. I can't take her to work as there are too many other dogs there.'

'I don't care. Deal with it.' He strode away, but the music didn't come back on.

Mollie found herself shaking. There was nothing for it; she had to take Mutantmutt with her. She would go via the vets and get that spray, plus anything else they could offer. It seemed to work that afternoon, and the other dogs, apart from sniffing at the incarcerated hound, didn't seem to twig about the season. The spray had worked. Ratty spent the afternoon guarding her imprisoned friend. The arrangement continued for the next few days, despite Mutantmutt's increasing amorousness. Mollie heaved a sigh of relief each day when she got home and counted the days until it was over. Soon the first mares would arrive, and the thought of that complication was too much.

Friday arrived with the prospect of an entire weekend off as it was still early season, and things were moving along at a pre-weekend pace at the yard. Liz was getting ready to take a ride out. Having got three excited kids mounted, she was preparing to leave. Mollie was checking the last stirrup leather when she heard a car coming down the lane, much too fast and in high revs. Gravel sprayed out from under its wheels as it careered into the yard. The driver had misjudged the bend. This had the effect on the waiting horses, who were already keyed up for their outing, to start playing up. The two cobs jumped and barge into each other and give each other a good kicking. The bay mare thought that actually, she fancied a snack in her box, and snatching the reins from the inexpert rider, she bolted into her box. This was not helped by the stupid kid screaming. In the midst of this, the driver stopped the car, got out, and began bellowing at the top of his voice.

'I've had enough of you and your stupid dogs; I can't even get out of my front door now. There are at least two mutts barking and trying to get into your garden through my place.' It was James, his face red with fury. 'Do something about it now!'

This was the last straw for Liz's horse, a dizzy child of Keith's. She reared up and then expertly dropped her neck as her forelegs came to the ground and bucked. Liz stood no chance without a cowboy saddle with something to grip on. She flew out of the saddle and fell to the ground, catching her hat on the mounting block, wrenching her neck and shoulder with the full force of the fall.

From nowhere came all the stable girls, the noise and the sounds of screaming having alerted them. Horses were expertly caught, kids dismounted, and the situation dealt with. This left Mollie as the first aider to deal with Liz, who lay unconscious on the ground. She was breathing, but the odd angle she was lying at left Mollie unsure whether to move her into the recovery position. Having rung the ambulance, she fetched a rug from a stable door and laid it over Liz, who now began to groan.

'Liz, it's Mollie, what's hurting?'

'Arrrrrrgghhhhhh.' From that, Mollie continued to talk to Liz, reassuring her all the horses and riders were fine but didn't move her further. At last, she could hear the sirens and the ambulance drove into the yard. It was only then that she noticed that James and his car had disappeared. Just as well, before she took to him with a pitchfork.

The efficient paramedics soon had Liz on a body board, with a neck brace and her limbs firmly secured, and they drove away. Suddenly the anti-climax hit Mollie, and she sat on the block feeling exhausted. The girls now came out of the stables where they had been pretending to sort the horses and kids, but were really keeping well away from the drama. They stood around Mollie, firing questions at her.

'What do we do now? What are her injuries? The kids are in the tack room. Do we do the three o'clock ride?' They were actually asking Mollie, she who they mocked, who was the laughing stock, and it fired her up. Just for once, she was in charge.

'Right, Sue, can you take the three o'clock? You others tack up. I'll call the parents of these kids and get them to come and collect them. Then we'll do stables as usual and I'll go to the hospital after we've locked up.' Then Mollie realised Liz might have had the key in her jodhs. She went into the office to see. Without Liz's presence, the room just seemed an untidy mess, but Mollie found the spare keys on a hook and the precious diary with phone numbers. There was going to be some explaining to do to parents...

Mollie made her way down the hospital corridor, counting the numbers on the doors, her sense of dread growing with each footfall. 'Just how bad was Liz? Would she realise it was all her fault?' Cautiously, she knocked and went in room 35. Four beds and in the far corner, Liz, rigged up to drips and monitors, was on her phone.

'Yes, of course, as soon as I have my diary. I'll ring you back and I'll book your daughter in. Thanks so much for your call.' She looked up to see Mollie. 'Ah, good, my diary! Did you lock up with the spare keys?' Mollie, in her astonishment, just nodded and handed the book over.

'They say I've broken four ribs, and I've got to stay here until they stabilise and they're sure they're not going to damage my lungs. Dammed nuisance, but we'll keep going.' Despite her brisk words, Liz was as white as a sheet.

'Now, you'll have to take charge of things for the moment. After work each day, I'll need you to pop in and we'll go through the following day's appointments. I can still order the feed and bedding, but you'll need to let me know when things are getting low. Wages I can do online, but you'll have to bring in the timesheets. You don't need to do anything with the paperwork in the office. I have my own system, so please don't touch it.' She seemed to have thought everything through in such a short time. 'I'd like to get my hands on that prat in the car and wring his neck. Wrong turning, I suppose. These idiots from the town.'

She didn't know, she hadn't heard the tirade, or had forgotten it. Hopefully, it would remain so. Mollie heaved an inward sigh of relief.

'What about when I have to take the mares up to the farm? Won't that leave us shorthanded? I can't take your hacks and do that, too. None of the others can lead out yet.'

'That's a point. I'll have to think about that one.' Mollie was tempted to ask if she would get a wage rise, but didn't quite have the courage; still full of guilt. Liz tried to turn in the bed but gasped in pain and reached to turn one of the monitors up. Just then, the phone rang, and Mollie could see her deciding which was more important. The phone won. In a hoarse voice, she took a booking for the weekend.

'Give me a couple of minutes and I'll let you know what tomorrow has. You'll have to bring one of the spare diaries, so you can keep a record. Here's a page of mine.' She upped her dose, then proceeded to dictate, not only the whole day, but who should ride each horse as if Mollie couldn't work it out? Her voice got slower and slower as she got to the end of the list. The extra painkillers were kicking in. 'Now I think I'll have a little snooze.' Her eyes shut, and she was out of it. Mollie got up and left, but as she shut the door, she heard that interminable ring tone start again.

The dogs were waiting patiently in the car; no bickering, as Mollie had put one in the front, the other in the back. Deep in thought, Mollie drove wearily home. She could see a long, hard summer in front of her. Liz had looked so ill, it surely must be weeks before she could get out, let alone ride? She would also have to deal with James. The way he had behaved was intolerable. So what if he was a tenant? If it wasn't for her parents, she'd send him packing right now. As she turned the corner, she saw there really were two dogs outside the house, but it was her door, not his. She got out of the car and growled at them. When this had no effect, she ran at them, shouting, and this finally had some effect, as they slunk away down the street, looking over their shoulders all the way. She knew who owned them; she would ring them later. The lights were on in James' side, but she was suddenly just too hacked off to face him. In the morning would do.

James saw the lights of Mollie's car just as he was writing the last sentence. Finished. His best book for a long time, written in record time despite the hindrances. In fact, taking himself out in the car had increased his flow to the conclusion. Tomorrow he would email his masterpiece to his publisher, then pack and take himself off to France for that long-promised holiday. He saw the dogs had gone. Good, so all was in order, but maybe he had been a bit rash going down to the stable yard. Perhaps if he went around with the bottle of champagne he had bought for this event, she might forgive him and might even succumb to his deadly charm. He grinned at himself in the hall mirror as he let himself out.

Mollie was feeding the dogs when the doorbell rang. Unprepared, she answered the door to find a grinning James. All her anger welled up and she was about to give him what for when he spoke. 'I'm so sorry about this afternoon. I really must apologise. I was so near finishing my book and I was in a bit of a state!' He waved the bottle under her nose. 'Here are my apologies. Do join me; I've finished the book and you'll soon have your peace and quiet back!'

Taken aback by the apology and not given a chance to reply, Mollie found herself being pushed by James' presence back into the kitchen. The dogs had finished stuffing their faces and looked at him. They still weren't sure of him and took themselves to the sofa for a snooze, but not a deep one, their eyes now and then opening to check things out.

'Now let's get the party started!' laughed James. He waltzed past Mollie and opened the back door. He eased the cork out of the bottle. 'Quick, some glasses!' Mollie automatically reached for a couple of mugs, and as the bottle popped, James poured liberal portions into each one. He then sat at the table and took a huge swig. 'Come on, drink up! Here's to my new book, which is going to outsell all the others, and my holiday which begins tomorrow!' Bowled over, Mollie took her own huge swig, which went straight to her head, not her stomach, as she hadn't eaten all day.

'Now tell me all about yourself!' James demanded.

'There's not much to say, just teaching riding and running this place for my parents.'

'Great… Do you know, I think this is my best work yet? Let me tell you the plot, you see there's this…'

Mollie was regaled with the intricate details of what seemed to her a really boring story about someone finding themselves through life and love. Not at all original, but who was she to say? She slurped on her champagne, which she didn't really like, and which James kept on topping up. Soon her head was spinning, and she just wanted to sleep. James was rooting around in the cupboard and found another bottle of white, which he opened and poured liberally.

THREE

Mollie was woken by the sound of a car being driven out of the garage and the dogs barking in protest. 'Thank heavens I don't have to get up!' She looked at the clock and saw it was indeed Saturday, but it was only 5 a.m. Then she remembered bits of last night and saw the dented pillow beside her. Oh, no, she'd done it again. The shame and filth waved across her yet again. When would she learn to say no and mean it? At least there would be no walk of shame. He was gone, no one to face up to and be let down by. No one who would know and snigger behind her back. She would have to live with herself. Again, she felt sullied and dirty. The dogs had shown their disgust by sleeping downstairs. She was alone again. Was it ever going to end? Others could find people that stuck; why not her? Was there something intrinsically amiss with her that she picked the losers and got used by them? She struggled out of the entwined sheets and shuffled to the shower. The phone rang.

'I know it's a bit early, but I guess you must be about with the dogs and all that. They had us up at the crack of dawn here with thermometers and blood pressure things.' Who else but Liz? A new wave of dread engulfed Mollie; it was work today, no weekend off. 'A couple of things I thought of. It was a good thing I let you keep the keys, as you'll need to have the office open to do the payments. At least you know how to use that machine. The cash box is locked in the cupboard at the back. I usually empty it each night and keep it in the flat. I'll have to get my husband to pop in and fetch it, so it isn't in the office each night.'

Mollie started thinking fast, despite a hovering headache. 'But I can't do all the transactions and take rides and bookings and do all the other things; it's just not possible!'

'I can see your point. I really will see if I can get the landline converted to go to the mobile; that's one thing. My husband might be able to help out. I'll get back to you. Ohh, breakfast.'

'Husband, Liz had a husband?' No one had ever seen him if so, but there was another door to the flats, or maybe she kept him locked in? Mollie really needed that shower now and the hot water helped to get the brain cells working. She would walk the dogs and leave them at home. No one to annoy. Sam, the cleaner, would be in by lunchtime and would let them out before and after her work. One less thing to worry about. She dressed rapidly. Liz's call at least meant she had plenty of time to get to the yard. She marched the dogs down the fields to the river, thinking and planning frantically as she read the work list for the day. It certainly cleared her head. Last night was just a blip. He was gone; it could all be forgotten; put it down as a warning to start afresh whenever her social life started again. She actually had no choice.

Back home, she popped into next door to see what the place was like. What greeted her was a mixture between a disaster zone and a bomb site. The place was littered with food wrappers, empty bottles and ashtrays which were full of cigarettes that looked like reefers. It would take weeks to get rid of the smell; the house was strictly no smoking. She'd best call Sam and warn her. Whatever she couldn't finish, Mollie would have to sort in the next few days. The kitchen bin was overflowing, and when Mollie opened the fridge, the smell nearly knocked her out. So much untouched food. The bathroom looked like a plague of footballing teenagers had been in. She couldn't face the bedroom but reached for her phone and took shots around the place. Her parents wouldn't be able to argue the extra cleaning time when they saw these. She salvaged a few of the edibles and left the rest for Sam. Cleaner's perks. On her way out, Mollie saw her favourite old hunting print stuck by the front door and returned it to its place. Time to go; she couldn't linger.

The yard seemed to be in a sort of new light as Mollie parked the car. Her tiredness evaporated into a brisk purposefulness that she'd never experienced before. She'd gone onto a sort of overdrive and it was a great feeling. This lasted only until she went into the feed room, ducking the whinnies to find that none of the feeds had been made up. Cursing, she rushed through, having to miss out some of the ingredients because no one had soaked the sugar beet or the bran. Hopefully, one day wouldn't hurt. She was just heaving the last pile of buckets onto the yard when the girls arrived.

'Who didn't make the feeds up last night, Tina?'

'We usually do it when we arrive on the Saturdays when you're… not here.'

'And you got away with it? Didn't the dragon notice? Poor horses. Tina go and feed the last lot; then we'll meet in the tack room.'

Tina slunk off and Mollie went to fill the kettle, making sure there was enough water in it for once. The other two followed in unusual silence. Coffee made in silence, they hovered until Tina returned.

'Right, Liz has broken four ribs and will be in hospital for several weeks. I may know more tonight. I had it dumped on me to run things. I will have to take payments and most of the things Liz does, except shout and scream.' Mollie hoped this pre-planned speech would work. 'I have to go to the hospital each evening, so Tina, you will have to lock up. I have both sets of keys. I know you don't like me, but we've got to work together, or we'll all be out of a job when she returns.' Mollie noticed the sideways, shifty looks. On cue, her phone rang.

'I hope you've fed. The first hack is at 10.30. You must make sure that Mouse has the martingale on for the Spencer kid, she always winds him up and he won't stop without some form of head control.' Mollie knew all this but nodded and clucked to the tirade with a grimace on her face. After all, if Liz was ill and on a lot of painkillers, who was she to remind her that they all knew this? She let Liz run her course and rang off.

'Thank your lucky stars she won't be ringing you! Look, can we work together? We can change some things while she's not here, but it'll all be back to how it was when she returns unless we stand together.'

'What do you mean?' asked Alice.

'No morning tea break? How about no tack cleaning until the horses are finished for the day rather than having to be seen in here all the time with a sponge? Together we could nip through it in no time.'

'We could just rinse the bits,' ventured Heather.

'You're getting me!'

'Doing stirrups and girths in the school rather than the yard, so we don't have to do it twice?' grinned Tina.

'You get me absolutely! So how about now, we turn out all those who aren't being used this morning, rather than leaving them hungry in the stable?'

As a team, they scrutinised Mollie's list and then went to carry it out. The day wasn't all plain sailing, as they found some sense in Liz's rules. They turned Shamrock out, forgetting how difficult she was to catch if she was in the field on her own. In the end, they had to turn two others out before they got near her, but the pair then decided this was a good game and took off, too. Mollie was swamped by a wave of weariness.

'We could just open the gates and the stable doors; they'll come belting in,' suggested Sue, who usually had little to say for herself. They all looked at each other.

'Let's go for it!' Mollie went back and opened the stable doors and yelled when she was ready. The girls opened the gate and walked back. It was nerve-wracking for a minute; then there was a pounding of hooves and the three galloped past and into their boxes. Success!

'Thanks Sue. That was a real help.' Mollie was surprised to see her blush. Always the quietest in the team. Perhaps she had undisclosed depths!

Then came another of the frequent phone calls. Mollie just let Liz have her say and ignored most of it. Tack was cleaned in an hour when they worked out a team tactic of who did what. This meant that the horses were all tucked up, and the girls were all ready to leave at the official leaving time, not half an unpaid hour later. Mollie locked up and made her way to the hospital. Now to face the dragon. There had been few yard calls. She must have re-directed the line, which was a relief, but collecting the fees had been a real pain in the neck.

Opening the door to the hospital room, Mollie was surprised to see four very elderly ladies and no Liz. As she turned, there was a nurse behind her.

'We had to move Mrs Cox to a single room, as her phone was annoying the other patients. She's just across the corridor.'

'Thanks. I know I'm not family, but I work for her. Do you have any idea how long she's going to be in?'

The nurse grinned ruefully. 'I think she would like to be out tomorrow, but until she is stable, free of pain and able to move about easily, she has to stay put. I think at least a couple of weeks. I can't say anymore!' She backed away before Mollie could ask any more questions. Now she could hear Liz barking down the phone, so she entered carefully and sat down. Oh, for a cuppa. She glanced at her watch and hoped tonight's lecture wouldn't be too long.

'Ah, good to see you here promptly. How did today go?'

'Very well, the girls have pulled together, and the only real problem was the money taking, as I kept the 2.30 ride waiting, and then when we got back, the next lot were waiting to pay.'

'Right, we can't have that tomorrow. I'll send Peter to help; maybe the two of you can work it out.' Liz smiled. Mollie braced herself. 'We have two mares coming in the afternoon, and they'll need to go straight to Chris's. I've sorted a ride order out. If you go straight after the 3 o'clock lesson, you should be back to lock up.'

'Will we have to unload and then load again? It's not good for the mares.'

'It's a large lorry that won't go up the lane. Look, I've written it all out, so it should be plain sailing.' Again, that abnormal smile.

The door opened and to Mollie's horror, a policeman walked in.

'Mrs Cox? We need to fill out your statement; would you be able to do this now?'

'I don't see why not. Why the insurance needs all this, I don't know. Mollie, you'll have to do one, too.'

'What?'

'Well, it's a case of dangerous driving. We have the car description and we hope to find the driver quickly.'

Mollie wanted to curl up in a little ball under the bed and stay there. 'Yes, of course, but I can't give a lot of details. I didn't really see much.'

'I'm sure you'll be surprised by how much you recall. If I give you this form, would you like to do it now?' As if she had any choice. Mutely, Mollie took the board and began filling in her details. She couldn't lie, could she? Or just by omission? Not give any details, like the driver was my tenant? She sucked on the pen. Maybe it was get your own back time? She put pen to paper, writing a very careful description of the car with its dented wing. Surely that would be enough? No, she couldn't do it, but she wasn't going to come clean in front of Liz. She ended it with saying that she thought it was her tenant, but couldn't be sure as she had been dealing with the emergency and he had left the next day. She looked at the policeman.

'Could we just go over this? Maybe leave Liz to write in peace?' He caught her glance and nodded. In the corridor, she handed him the clipboard and waited while he read it.

'Why didn't you say anything before?'

'I wasn't aware it was a police matter, and I cannot be entirely sure.'

'Well, this changes things. And is Mr Whitaker still in your cottage?'

'No, he's left. He lives somewhere on the other side of London. I have the details at home.'

'If you could ring the station with those details?'

'Yes, of course, but one thing, could you keep my part in this away from Liz for the moment, if not permanently?' Mollie tried her best big, soppy eye look. 'She is, um, quite difficult to work for, and I have to deal with running the yard and everything until she's better. I'm not worried about what happens to Mr Whitaker. After all, if I had rung Crime stoppers or something like that, it would be….' He actually smiled. 'I'll do my best, but I can't promise anything.'

'Thank you, I'm really grateful. I'd better go back in for the rest of my orders.'

He followed her in, took Liz's statement and was gone. Liz went through the list, barked more orders, which went right through Mollie as she knew she was running on empty, and she was gone as fast as her tired feet could take her.

The dogs were so pleased to see her, Mutantmutt

now well out of season, back to her normal noisy self. Mollie slumped in the garden as they rushed around, realising it was nearly 8 and it would be another hectic day tomorrow. The dogs came rushing up, both trying to sit on her lap and she just let them smother her in licks, slobber and hair. Emotions whirled around in her, having been kept back all day, and she couldn't pin on any single one at any moment. Maybe she actually had to take a leaf out of her mother's book, which was to batten it all down, bury it and just carry on, like that stupid advertising gimmick. In some ways, the day on the yard had been a pleasant surprise, but would it last?

FOUR

'I don't see why you should have all the say in who's taking the rides out.' Tina stood with hands on hips, her body language furious. 'That kid has never ridden Clover, and he's far too strong for her.'

'Look, I'm sorry; I have Liz's list and we must go with it, even though I agree.'

'But as I keep on telling you. She. Won't. Know.'

'And I say it is just sod's law that she will, and I'm not having the poop thrown at me.'

'And who put you in charge of us, anyway? I've been here longer than you, and I'm better qualified.'

'You are not. You're still doing your stage 4 and I've had that for five years, and you can't drive.'

'Where had Tina got this idea?' she thought

Tina scowled. Mollie sighed. 'I'll ring Liz and explain, OK?'

Mollie's forebodings had been right; the team work wouldn't last. This morning had been nothing but grumps and complaints. The girls had arrived with this agenda on board, and she suspected Tina was behind it all. 'Just what was her problem?' She dialled.

'Hi Liz, we have just been discussing the 10.30 ride and Tina isn't happy with Tom riding Clover.'

The blast from the phone had her holding it at arm's length, and Tina could hear exactly what Liz thought. She slinked off to the tack room before Liz had finished. After Liz had finished the tirade, Mollie followed Tina. This couldn't go on.

'Look, Tina, I didn't ask to be put in charge. It was just assumed, and the dragon won't run it any other way. I'm sorry, but we must be open and do it all above board; or if there is a problem, then we might all lose our jobs. Look, take a lead rein with you and if Clover does mess about, use that.'

Tina was still scowling.

'Look, Tina, we have to work together while she's incarcerated. Then you can tell her exactly how you feel or go to the hospital yourself and talk to her now. I can't do any more than this, and I'm no happier than you about the situation.'

'Oh, I suppose so. I'll work with you, but I don't like you, and I will tell Liz how I feel. I don't care what you say; I should have been in charge, as I've been here longer. You don't know anything.' She stalked out of the tack room. Mollie sat for a minute, all the beneficial effects of a good night's sleep vanishing. She felt totally drained. She hated the feeling of having to work with someone now so openly hostile, but she was trapped. Mollie heard hooves on the yard and went out to help with tacking up. One of the dads was watching. She went over to him.

'Hi, I was wondering if you need to pay? The office is over here.'

He turned, and Joanna felt for the first time ever in her life that bit in all the books where your stomach turns, and you go dizzy and feel like gasping for air. 'So, it was true. He wasn't even that good looking, so what was wrong with her? He was older, slightly plump, with cropped greying hair. Nothing special.'

'Oh, hi, you must be Mollie,' he smiled. 'I'm Liz's husband, Peter.'

Mollie knew she couldn't be a goldfish and shut her mouth as her spirits sank. She gave her hand. 'Correct. Liz sent you to help with the payments?'

'Yes, if you'll show me how and where I can crack on. I'll be here until you finish, and I'll pay the cash in tonight, so you can go straight to the hospital.'

Mollie tried smiling. No one could ever know how her heart was somersaulting. 'Was she sixteen again? She led him to the office and, taking a grip, showed him the system and where Liz's supply of coffee was. He was so nice, didn't get cross with her when the cash machine crashed and it took ages to get it working again. It was such a relief not to be bamboozled by someone barking out orders and then getting cross when she explained something unclearly. How could he be married to such a difficult woman?

'So, I think that's everything; are you ok? It's such a relief to not have to do this anymore. Will you be here during the week?'

'No, have to work, but I'll be in the office for

at least the next couple of weekends until Liz is home. I'll be here to help with the mayhem!' His grin had her weak at the knees. She couldn't cope with this. Mollie was out of the office and back on the yard. The morning was calmer than its start; Liz only rang four times, repeating instructions and then relaying them through Peter, which in turn had Mollie even more harassed than normal. The rides went out, Clover did misbehave, and Tina smiled triumphantly at her when she dragged the pony back in. Mollie had to diffuse the situation.

'Should I send her a photo?' She managed a smile.

'No, but you just tell her tonight the little swine nearly bolted on the common.'

'Not good, but was everything else OK?'

'Fine, but Dazzler has a loose shoe. He'll need the farrier.'

'Will ring him.' Anything to keep things defused. Mollie grabbed her phone. Just after the ponies were fed and everyone was heading to the tack room to eat, a large transporter turned up. Mollie's heart sank. The mares were early.

'Made really good time,' smiled the driver. 'Shall we unload straight away?'

'Are they good for a couple of minutes while I get our trailer hitched? We can do a straight on and off.'

'Might be a good idea; the little grey can be a swine in small trailers.'

As Mollie was driving into the yard, Liz rang again and so she had to tell her about the mares.

'Well, just make it a nice, brisk job. Move them swiftly from one to the other. No nonsense, you mind.' Then more to the same effect. Eventually, Mollie rang off, and they got the ramp down opposite the trailer and put the side gates up. The little bay mare was sweet; there was enough room to turn her in the transporter and Mollie led her down. She followed like a lamb and was soon secured. Not so easy with the grey. Bill, the driver, pushed her slowly backwards, so he could turn her, and she resisted with a half rear. He talked to her and soothed her and eventually she agreed to turn, but as soon as she saw the other box, her ears pricked up and she began to snort fiercely and stamp her feet.

Mollie's phone rang, and she turned away to answer. Liz, of course. 'Got them loaded, then?' Her voice seemed louder than normal. 'No, the second one is being skittish. I must go and help.' Mollie put the phone down with more courage than she'd felt for ages.

'Shall I get some carrots?' she offered.

'We can but try.'

The mare sniffed the carrots but wouldn't have anything to do with them, wasn't hungry. She continued her halt at the top of the ramp and wasn't going to budge. They tried side lines, pulling lunge rope around her quarters, but that pony was fixed. Then Mollie had an idea. 'Shall

I take the trailer further away, then maybe we can mob walk her in?' The pony was only about fourteen hands. Mollie's phone rang again, and by the time she had finished, Bill had moved the trailer around the corner and was ready for another try. The noise had alerted all around, and now not only the staff, but assorted kids and Peter were watching the show.

She now allowed herself to be led down the ramp, but not without a lot of snorting and shaking her head. Bill kept the momentum going around the corner, but as soon as she saw the trailer, her head went up and her feet were glued to the ground.

'I knew this was a bad idea,' moaned Bill. 'I'm sure the transporter could get most of the way up the lane.'

'But it would be scratched to bits and there's a nasty bend.'

'Stuff the animal.'

'Let's march her in,' suggested Mollie desperately. 'There's loads of people here now.'

'I'll try any flipping thing!' Bill laughed.

Mollie explained to all about putting the lunge line around the horse, all grabbing it as if in a tug of war but keeping so close that the mare couldn't kick. The team was sorted, with key players on the dangerous end, and they marched upon the horse. The onslaught was so swift they actually caught her out and she found herself halfway up the ramp before she could think of a new ruse. Then Mollie's phone went off. In that split second, everyone was slightly diverted and the mare, with lightning reactions, reared and, knocking half the team over, was off the ramp and back on the ground, still snorting. Mollie ignored the call, but her phone kept ringing.

'For heaven's sake, turn the ringtone down!' snapped Tina. Mollie did so, but inadvertently answered it.

'What the dickens hell is going on? Why aren't you keeping me updated?' yelled Liz. Mollie found her phone snatched from her hand by Peter.

'You stupid woman, we'd just got the daft animal halfway up the ramp and you ruined it. Now we've got to start all over again...' He put the phone down, turned it down and handed it back to an open-mouthed Mollie. 'What a man.' He proceeded to take things over.

'Right, team, let's do this again, but this time the men at the back, you two big girls at the front and the rest of you heave at the sides. Now, one, two, three, go!'

The manpower at the back worked and the resisting horse was walked by sheer bullying and tied to the front of the trailer before she could issue a snort. The group backed up rapidly and pushed the inner door to. The mare snorted again, but it was defeated.

'Thank you, Peter, that was ' Mollie looked her hero in the eye. 'How come you've never been to the yard before? We could have done with your ideas on other things!!' She wasn't going to mention the Liz silencing.

'Can't stand horses, and Liz can't stand estate agents, so we keep work separate!' he laughed. 'Now anyone need to pay me for their ride?'

Bill and Mollie closed the trailer.

'Will Liz ring me when they're done?'

'I guess so. I never explained why she's not here; she's in hospital!'

'That explains a lot. When I come to collect them, I'll bring our trailer and go straight there. If there had been any injuries, we wouldn't have heard the end of it.' They grinned conspiratorially. 'Why Liz insisted we bring the transporter, I'll never know. Now, will I be paid in the usual way?'

'You'd better check with Peter; not my department!'

Driving up the hill, Mollie pondered the morning's events. It all felt like a lot of weight on her. She had no confidence in her ability to deal with Tina. She would have to find the way to not only be firm but also friendly. Could she do that with all that hostility? And Peter, all she admired in a man, standing up to Liz, organising things successfully; someone to lean on. Married. Unfair. She would just have to stamp on this crush. It could only lead to complications and was a nonstarter. No, not even in your imagination, woman!

It was almost a relief to arrive at the farm to Chris's quiet calm. Both mares unboxed easily; his steady hand with the animals calming the grey as she shot backwards out of the box from hell. Thankfully, the shoes were already off, so they just had to take all the travel bandaging off.

'Nice couple of mares; this will take Keith's mind off causing trouble.'

'What's he done now?'

'Well, he covered both my mares and things got boring. He took himself over the fence to next door's shire mare.'

'He didn't?'

'He did.'

Mollie felt a wave of exhaustion. 'Have you told Liz? You know about the accident?'

'Oh, yes, I had a phone call the day after, and now she phones me for updates.'

'She wouldn't have done that normally; must be the drugs! She's on at me all the time.' Mollie remembered her phone and switched it back on. Ten missed calls from guess who, but she wasn't going to call her back and she even put the call to silent.

'And about Keith?'

'Not flipping likely. The mare has just retired, and their kids are over the moon about the idea of a foal in the spring. It seemed a fair deal with the broken fence... I'm not telling unless it turns out with identical Keith markings!'

Mollie's phone rang, and the guilt made her give in. 'Yes Liz, no Liz, I'm there now's fine, we're just turning the mares out now; I must go.' She put the phone down. New courage. They untied the mares and let them go. From over the hill came an imperious shout.

Meanwhile, James sat in the foyer tugging at his badly fitting, rumpled shirt. Still, with the advance royalty for the book, he could use the laundry again. Ava must also think it was going to be a bestseller, as she had rung him within two days of his emailing the manuscript, demanding a meeting, which was highly unusual. He fiddled with a magazine, but in his head he bought that yacht. At last, here she was, the usual cursory handshake, and he followed her in.

'Now James, I'm afraid we're not going to be going ahead with this book. The plot is non-existent, you change the main character's gender halfway through, and then add spurious wildlife description that has absolutely nothing to do with the plot. And what was it with the dogs that you killed?'

'Are you sure? This is the best thing I've ever written! Could you have muddled me with someone else?'

'Now, do you think I'm in the habit of making such mistakes? It was fine for about the first 10,000 words, but after that, it went haywire. You have two options. You go off and re-write, and it'll probably be another reasonable seller for you. It's nothing special. I can extend your deadline for another six weeks, if we're going to make the Christmas market. Or you can walk out of here and we will cancel the contract. You will continue to receive royalties, but we won't publish you again.'

James went hot and cold. He couldn't believe all this was true. 'Pass me the printout; maybe I mailed the wrong file.' He knew he was clutching at straws. He turned to the middle after checking that the first page was his, and as he read, he felt dizzy and tired. It was rubbish. In places, complete nonsense.

'I guess I have to get back to work,' he mumbled and staggered out of the office, his world reeling.

FIVE

'I'm sorry; it's just all too much. I can't go on like this!' Mollie was in meltdown. 'I've worked six weeks through without a break; every stinking evening on to the hospital; twelve hour day. Then I have to deal with all of the problems here, work out each day's work with the girls. I've tried so hard to keep them on board and negotiate a good work day, but they all argue with everything I say, and then phone Liz behind my back, when it's her orders in the first place. Then I get it in the neck from her in the evening. They get days off, but when I ask, it's Oh, no, you must be here. I can do it; you can too; it's all about the calling to work with horses. If Tina is so darn keen that she is better than me, then why can't she cover for me? All those trips with those flaming mares up and down that lane. What do I have to do, get a sick note from the doctor? I'm so tired; I'm sick of horses. Can't you get her to do something? Why is she so long in hospital?'

Peter sat down beside her on the office sofa. 'I know, you've worked like a Trojan, but it's not for much longer. It's any day now. Ribs are difficult to heal, and she broke so many of them. I'm sure once she's out, she'll be straight up here, and she'll see what a brilliant job you've been doing,' he placated.

Mollie was still snottily sobbing into her tissues, but the tears were abating. She'd got over her crush on Peter in the past few weeks, as she'd seen how he was at the beck and call of Liz, getting almost as much stress as she had over the phone. It somehow diminished him in her eyes. She was well and truly off men. However, he was now putting his arm around her shoulder, which was a huge comfort, but started the tears afresh.

'So, this is what has been going on behind my back!' Framed like Cruella De Vil, Liz stood in the doorway, her silhouette expressing nothing but anger. 'It's just as well I decided to come straight here and not go home!'

'Nothing is going on!' shouted Peter to Mollie's surprise. 'You have overworked this woman for the past six weeks and she's just reached her limit. Not everyone is a workaholic like you.'

'Yeah, right,' she sneered. 'Then why hasn't she told me?'

Mollie rose to her feet. 'I have been asking you every evening for the past month for a day off, and each time, you've dismissed me and refused.'

'You weren't serious; it's not forever. And now I find you with my husband. Everything Tina has been saying has been true. Yard not being run properly; complaints from the riders.'

'That's an out and out lie. Things have gone really well. The yard is immaculate, and the tack has never been better cleaned since I reorganised the system. Just go and look.' Wrong thing to say.

'So, you have been undermining me.'

'NOOO!' Mollie yelled. 'It was a group decision to help the day be more well run.' She omitted 'and go home on time.' No effect. Liz strode into the room and faced Mollie off.

'And that's not all!' She yelled back. 'It was your friend who caused the accident in the first place and you never said a word. It was the police who told me, and you should be held responsible because it was your poor dog management that caused the whole situation. '

Mollie took a physical and mental step back, but Liz was off again. 'In the light of all this, I'm giving you a month's notice. You'll have to get the yard back to how I like it before you go.'

'Oh, no you don't.' Mollie was now filled with righteous anger. 'We never actually signed a contract; I'm not bound by anything. I was paid yesterday. You can stick your job. Let Tina take over. She's a crap instructor and couldn't organise her way out of a paper bag. I've worked all these long hours for you, never a thank you, just a presumption that I want to be your slave and never have a life of my own. You're nothing but a narrow minded, controlling bully.'

'But you have to take the mares up to Chris.' Liz wasn't hearing a word Mollie was saying.

'Too late, Liz. You should have thought all this through before you sacked the slave. You'll have to find someone to take the 10.30 and Sue isn't here today. They all have time off, unlike some. Good bye, Peter, it was nice working with you, but you're a mug to live with this.' Mollie slung the diary and her keys on the desk and stormed out. Tina was on the yard, with her ever present sneer. Mollie was on a roll. She picked up two of the filled water buckets lined up ready for making feeds, and slung them over Tina, who screamed in surprise, then wailed like a banshee, scaring a couple of ponies tied up by the fence.

'Goodbye, bitch!'

Mollie got the dogs out of the stable and drove off in a manner reminiscent of a certain lodger. Going home, she went between hysterical laughter and wanting to cry again, yet most of all was an overwhelming sense of relief. She was free of them all. No more stress. Liz, Tina, she wouldn't even miss the horses. She stopped at the shop and filled up on junk food for a lazy afternoon. The dogs were pleased at the smell of food.

To her surprise, there was a strange car parked outside the house. She wasn't expecting guests. Even worse, the front door was open. Leaving the dogs in the car, she went in. Her heart sank as she saw her parents standing in the hall.

'Ah, Mollie,' said her dad, as if he had been expecting her all along. 'Glad we've caught you. Got some news and a spot of bother.' Her mother appeared and gave her a perfunctory two sided peck. 'Let's not beat about the bush. Mr Whitaker has come to us with a terrible allegation! He says he left a Monet picture here when he left, and he wants it back. We've looked, but there's no sign of it.'

'There was no such picture here; the only thing I remember is that the hunting print was in the hall, and there was a space as if he'd hung something in the sitting room, but it wasn't there. Have you looked down the back of the sideboard?'

'Yes, yes, we've done all that. Do you think Sam could have taken it?'

'No, I checked the place before she arrived. It wasn't there. He did not leave any picture here!' Mollie was for the first time in her life standing up to her mother. 'Maybe we should all go and have another look together; I'm certain the picture isn't here.' She led the way and her parents actually followed. Over the next half an hour, they pulled furniture, threw cushions, opened and shut drawers, turned the bed on its sides, looked in the bins and even the compost heap.

'I give in, short of getting the cops in to verify it, I am certain the picture is not here,' said Mollie's dad a bit breathlessly. 'Now it's lunchtime and I need a beer.' He strode out of the house, and Mollie rushed to let the dogs out of the Land Rover into the house and then to catch her folks up. Once her dad had his pint, he seemed to calm down and her mother was her usual frosty self as they ordered a meal. Mollie had a sudden sense there was something else behind all this. She hadn't seen them in over a year and they had only spoken briefly on the phone and sent the odd text.

'So how much is this picture worth to bring you all the way down here?'

'Would you believe, about £100,000!'

'And he didn't even notice he had forgotten it for several weeks? Good grief!'

'Yes, he is a bit of an odd chap,' sighed her father. 'He's been a pain in the neck; but now we've checked it out, I hope he'll stop constantly ringing us.'

'I'm surprised he hasn't been down here himself,' said Mollie, feeling thankful.

'He's in the USA, apparently.'

'His book must have sold well!'

'Now there is another reason for us being here,' interrupted her mother. 'We've been thinking about what to do with this house, as you show no signs of settling down and it isn't making as much money as we expected.'

Mollie, as usual, rose to the bait. 'Mother, I'm only 23, give me a chance. And how many times have I asked you to give me autonomy to run the place as a Riders' B&B. But you just won't let me, and then you fill it with your snotty contacts at mate's rates. It's all your fault, not mine; I've done a good job.'

'That's as may be,' continued her mother undeterred. 'Your father and I want to do some travelling before it's too late, and we need to do some repairs to the house. We've sold the cottages to the Jarretts. Completion will be in six weeks, so you'll have plenty of time to find somewhere else. We'll give you something towards a deposit, but you've got a good job now, so you should have no problem. You can have your pick of the furniture.' She finished in a rush, having got it all out.

Mollie sat there in complete disbelief without a word to say. Talk about the icing on the cake. Mat pulled from under her feet. And expletives. She realised her parents were waiting for her reaction.

'Oh, right, fine. Yes, some money for the deposit would be good. How much were you thinking? 'She might be in robot mode, but she would need money until she found some work as well as a deposit on somewhere.

'Well, made a good profit, so five thousand?'

Mollie gulped mentally. 'That's not enough. I need at least £10,000 for a deposit,' she added. Her parents looked at each other, then nodded.

'Good, then it's all settled. So glad you were reasonable. We'll transfer the money as soon as we get the dough. I'll text you.' Her mother smiled rakishly. The attempt at humour fell flat on Mollie. Her father drained his glass. 'Right, we must hit the road. It's bridge tonight; do keep in touch.' They both air kissed Mollie and were on their way with unseemly haste. 'What had she done to deserve parents like this? Was there any chance she was adopted???' Mollie drained her glass and wandered home. She would take every single piece of furniture she could and flog it for something decent. The chances of her giving her parents her new home address were remote; they wouldn't notice, far less care.

SIX

Saturday morning arrived with sunshine and warm air. Mollie stretched her arms luxuriously and waited for the onslaught. It was as if the dogs thought alike, as within seconds they landed on her stomach and gave her a pre-rising wash. 'Down, you fools!' she laughed. Two days of complete rest, combined with a decision to take at least a week before doing anything at all, even think things through, had Mollie refreshed and full of energy. 'Right, you two nutters, do you know what today is?' Both dogs cocked their ears. 'It's Hazeley show today, and we're going! No horses to look after, just us three, and do you remember the dog food stall and the sausage stand?' Now their heads were on one side, as if they knew it was something good. 'Let's go!'

With more enthusiasm than she had had for ages, Mollie and the dogs leapt out of bed. She looked in the wardrobe. 'Just sod them all; I'll wear what I like, and no one is going to sneer!' She took out a bright blue pair of leggings and topped it with a psychedelic red and blue top. Perfect! They all bundled down the stairs, and the dogs raced around the garden while Mollie drank a swift cup of coffee. It was still early, but she knew the queues to get into the showgrounds began early. It also helped that she had a resident's pass for the wood car park and entrance. There were some benefits to living in Hazeley after all.

A few people were trickling in, and the grounds were relatively quiet. People were exercising horses; stall holders were finishing setting up and chatting to each other before the onslaught. Mollie avoided the horse section. Whether Liz had got her act together in such a short time was no longer her concern. No more sewing prickly plaits and brushing sticky hoof oil on; what a relief. Mollie headed to the food section. There was at least one dog food stall that would have freebies, but you had to be quick for them. Then it would be off to the breakfast bar for a sausage bap. Sheer heaven, and the dogs, on best behaviour, thought so, too, as they got free snacks from two stalls and a bite of Mollie's second bap! The three of them then went off to the crafts tent. This would be too busy for dogs later. Mollie found herself sighing at some landscape paintings. She would love to have a go at that, and hey, maybe now she could! That was a thought to hang onto. The next couple of hours had them tour all the tents, collecting freebies and advertising, all part of the fun to go through them all again in the evening. Listening to sales patter from various companies and even sitting in a new Land Rover was such a giggle, as she'd never part with hers. Well, at least the heater worked on it. They finished with the animal tents, admiring the cattle, sheep and pigs; the dogs politely sniffing through the bars, and not a single bark between them. Coming out into the fresh air, Mollie saw the great mobs had arrived and was glad she'd come early. Now she was going back to grab some lunch and sit in the stand to watch this year's display, which was the King's Troop horse artillery.

Walking along, she noticed something familiar about the couple in front of her. He was tall and blonde, wearing bright green trousers and a pink t-shirt – it could only be Chris! She didn't know the woman though, who was wearing jodhs and sweatshirt. Most interesting. At that moment, the couple swung around, nearly knocking into Mollie and the dogs. For a split second, Mollie and Chris made deep eye contact.

'Mollie, you made it after all! I'm so pleased!' To her horror, he then proceeded to air kiss her, but he muttered, 'help' in a frantic whisper in her ear. For once in her life reacting quickly, rising to the cue. 'I'm so sorry I'm late, overslept again. I was just going to ring and find out where you were!'

'No problem, as I was just saying to Jenny here, we had this date arranged for lunch! Jenny, I'm so sorry, maybe another time?' He smiled a huge, placating smile.

'Yes, of course. Maybe you'll come to the box after the show? We're having a party.' She also smiled a huge wistful smile and was gone.

'Over my dead body,' muttered Chris.

'What on earth was that all about?' Chris was

greeting the dogs.

'Every time I come to this show, I get all these women from the Riding Club hitting on me. It's bad enough if I meet them in the pub, but here they're worse for some reason!'

'Don't you like the attention, then?' Mollie grinned.

'Oh, it's all so shallow; I can't be bothered with it all,' he snorted. 'Look, would you do me a favour and come with me while I look around? At least I would be left in peace to look at things.'

Mollie wasn't sure if this was a compliment or an insult. 'I don't see why not, but I have already been around most things. I was just getting food, then going to watch the Kings Troop horse artillery display.'

'Is that soon, then?'

'Half an hour and the stand is filling up.'

'Right, here's the deal; let's get loads of food, watch that, so you get a rest, then we'll go around. The crowds are always a bit quieter at lunchtime.'

'It's a deal!' Mollie suddenly felt like some company.

They sat sharing sandwiches, crisps and beer with the dogs in the stand, then gasping and laughing at the brilliant display of horsemanship as the Troop galloped about the arena, cutting corners, galloping through each other's lines and finally getting the gun carts, then firing the guns in a salute. They then went around most of the tents and stands again, Chris' interest being in the cattle and the farm machinery. He proved a quiet companion, but his wry remarks had Mollie giggling like a teenager. There were at least three women giving her evil looks, too, which they laughed about as soon as the person was past. The day was ending as they made their way back to the main entrance.

'Thanks, you've made what was going to be irksome a really great day!'

'So why did you come, if it was going to be such a problem?'

'I needed a break from the farm and this was always my parents' most favourite day out. I do it to remember them. It's been five years since they went.'

He really looked sad, and Mollie, remembering the awful accident, suddenly found herself inviting him to join her at the beach. 'I'm going to Thorn's Beach tomorrow for a bit of fresh air, some quiet time.' Why was she doing this? It was her planning day, coming to grips with things day, and she didn't really want to share it.

'Wouldn't I be intruding?' he asked astutely. 'Not at all. We can picnic and just chill out, maybe have a paddle. I'm not hitting on you! You look like you still need a break!' Mollie had noticed that he was thinner than before, with shadows under his eyes.

'So just a quiet time with some sea air? Nothing else?'

'Believe me, nothing else, I need some seaside therapy and the dogs don't always have the right answer; sausages aren't the answer for everything!'

'But they go a good way!!'

'You really are welcome, but on one proviso! You must bring Rex. He needs some doggy play time away from guarding your farm!'

'Sorted! I don't have to milk until six, so we can make a day of it. Pick you up at 10?' Suddenly there seemed a change in the balance, but Mollie wasn't caring. 'I'll be ready with food!'

The sea air was just what she had needed. Mollie was lying on a blow-up mattress in the corner of a breakwater. The sun was hot, but a gentle breeze helped. All she could hear was the waves, the occasional sea gull, and Chris gently snoring. They had made their way down the gravel track in a peacefulness she hadn't expected. In fact, she had got cross with herself again when she got home for being so gutless, when she had really designated today for sorting her master plan out. She hadn't wanted any counsel but her own, but Chris had been quietly, unobtrusively cheerful and, with the dogs playing around them, all suddenly seemed fine. Of course, the glass of wine helped too, she sniggered to herself. Despite it being a Bank holiday weekend, there were very few people on this beach, as it wasn't signposted. Everything was just perfect. In half an hour, she really would begin to pull herself together. Really.

Chris suddenly sighed and sat up. 'I'm going for a swim. You, too?'

'No, I've had my annual paddle.' He was up and gone as if he was running from something and threw himself into the sea. Ratty, Mutantmutt and Rex leapt in, too, with excitement, but they couldn't keep up with him and resorted to bouncing around with each other at the edge. Lazily, Mollie sat up and watched the action. Chris continued swimming up and down and diving in and out of the waves. Idly, she looked at him. No, he wasn't her type, if there was one. Too thin, no broad shoulders despite the farm work, and his blonde hairlessness had a pinkness about it that she found a bit revolting. Of course, he was pleasant to talk to, but nothing. No. She couldn't see what the riding club ladies saw in him. He made his way out and fought off the excited dogs to flop on the rug.

'Penny for them?' Mollie knew she was blushing, but knew her curls were covering her face. 'My nanny used to bring me here, too.'

He squinted at her. 'But you weren't brought up here?'

'No, Winchester. I moved here when my parents bought the cottages and talked me into running one of them for holiday lets. Did I tell you what they've done now?' She couldn't help but let the anger into her voice. 'They've only gone and sold them. I have to be out in six weeks! I begged them to let me run it properly, but oh no, they just used it for all their sick and stupid friends and made no money on the cottage and then blamed it on me!' Her voice was rising, but it was like the dam was breaking.

'Then I got the sack; I mean, Chris, talk about the rug being pulled from under my feet!'

'OMG, tell all.'

She did, finding a real relief in finally talking to someone about it, not a dog. At the end she pulled herself together, relieved. 'So, I have six weeks to find a new home and job! But actually, I'm finding, apart from all the injustice of it, I feel quite free! Thanks for listening!'

'I've never been a confidante before!' He grinned. 'I think you should make a revenge plan; how to ruin the stables or make the cottages fall down – after you've left, of course!' He took a swig of his beer. 'But I have an idea that might suit us both. It's only just forming, so let me witter... I need some help around the farm. It would be nice to have a morning off from milking.'

Mollie snorted, 'I've never been near a cow in my life!'

'But you do horses, and cows can be just as sweet, if a bit smellier! Hear me out. I just want a quiet life, and I do want to do more with the farm. But also, I want to go back to Bible College.'

'You? A priest?'

'No, not that sort, not Catholic. Free church, one that trains you as a missionary or a pastor or something that you're called to. I only keep the farm going for my parents. Maybe I need to sell it, but right now, I could do with some help... and there's the women thing. I will make my own moves in my own time. If you were around, they might back off, leave me in peace. They wouldn't have to know you were just helping out.'

Mollie sat up. 'This isn't a double bluff? You really mean just a house sharing, with no commitments? A compromise, but to the world we're together? But what if I finally meet someone? Not that it's likely every relationship I've had has been a disaster.' Mollie mused for a minute; she was seeing those dark brown eyes again, the bastard. 'It would be a relief for me, too. Let the world think things so, but really just housemates?'

'Yeah, think it through.'

'Could we store all my parent's furniture somewhere?'

'Plenty of room in the barn.'

'But I will need to find some work. I'll have my parent's money, and a little savings, but that won't last forever with rent to pay.'

Chris smiled, 'no rent, just costs.'

'You serious? So, I'd have time to find some work?'

'Absolutely.'

For a couple of minutes they were both deep in thought. The waves broke in a clichéd manner on the beach.

'I had actually just left for college when my

parents died. Hardly unpacked, not got my room sorted, not even my first timetable. Why they drove home on the motorway I'll never know. We'd gone over on the B roads...' His voice trailed off. 'But it's past history now, even if the pain still sometimes comes back.' Mollie put her hand on his; it was all she could manage. 'They'd found all the funds for me to go, even selling up most of the stud after I said I didn't want the farm.' Chris shook himself a bit like a small dog. 'So now, what do you think? Compromise living?'

'You know, I think it could work. I'm sorry, Chris, but I must say from the start, I'm not at all attracted to you, so there's not going to be a happy ending, if that's what you're looking for.' Blunt as ever Mollie.

'Works both ways. Good company. Like minded, maybe. No more Riding club bitches!!!' Conspiratorially, they laughed. Whatever they still had hidden, whatever the world might think, this was the compromise for now.

In a dark community hall in the dirty side streets of New York, a group of weary-looking people were setting up chairs in a circle, while a coffee machine chugged in the background. Finally, cups in hands, they sat and waited. Each looking at each other. inwardly willing the other to go first. Break the ice. Finally, the tall, scrawny guy with the odd accent cleared his throat and cleared it again. They all looked at him expectantly. He finally found the courage.

'Hi, my name's James. 'They all mumbled their names back and smiled. 'My name's James.' He said with more strength. 'I'm an addict to just about everything you can lay your hands on. I've drunk, smoked and injected everything I can find.' Some smirked in recognition of the case history. 'I've wasted a shed load of money, alienated myself from everyone who comes near me; I've abused and used. But today,' he choked back theatrical tears. 'But today, I've been clean for a month!' The gang stood and cheered and clapped him on the back.

SEVEN

Mollie lay in bed listening to the clatter of Chris's clogs as he came down the attic stairs in the early morning quietness. She really couldn't put this off any longer. She sat up and stretched, threw the quilt off with it narrowly missing the sleeping dogs. They looked up with bleary eyes, then snuffled back together. Too early for them. Rapid dressing was needed, and she shoved on her thickest jodhs jumper and ran down to the kitchen to find her wellies. It was thankfully warm in the kitchen, but she still rushed out into the early morning to keep warm. The trees were starting to turn and there was that hint of autumn in the air. Crossing the yard, Mollie noticed the hum of the milking machine and a steady clonking coming from the milking parlour.

She threw open the door and went in. The smell and warmth were a barrage on all senses. Cows, cow dung, fart, burp and breathing mixed with hay, grass and some sort of chemical. It was wonderful, completely unlike a stable, but welcoming and comforting. Chris was in t-shirt and jeans, with an odd stool thing belted around his waist. He smiled. 'Just watch for a while and see what I do. It's all quite simple, really.' So, Mollie leant against the wall and did just that.

She found herself fascinated as she followed the process through. First of all, Chris took a cloth from a bucket at the side and wiped the cow's udders down, then threw the used cloth into another bucket. He then got what she could only think of as a larger bucket with tubes and metal pipes attached to the narrow top and put it by the cow, who remained stoically munching on her hay. He fixed a long tube to a pipeline that ran along the ceiling. The four metal pipes now hissed, and he adroitly pushed one onto each teat, each seeming to be sucked on. Then began the clicking she had heard earlier, accompanied by an odd sort of squeak. Mollie gasped as she saw the milk coming down the clear plastic into the bucket. Chris now sat on the odd sort of thing on his waist and it all made sense. It was a one legged stool.

He took a small bucket from the side, quickly milked a few drips out into it, then took a tube of ointment and smeared this on the teats of the cow he had previously milked. Then they watched for a couple of minutes.

'This is a very old system, but it works. Dad spent years getting it to his satisfaction, so I'm not going to change it. Do you hear the sound changing?' Mollie moved over and saw the milk was no longer gushing and the squeak was now a squawk. Chris got up and unplugged the airline, but the teats stayed in place. He flipped a switch on the clicking thing and the teats dropped down, but he caught them before they hit the floor. 'A teat full of dung will ruin the whole bucket. Be aware!' He lifted the contraption and went to the back of the dairy. Here he flipped the handle over the bucket, releasing the cluster, which he put on a clean bench. He then tipped the milk into a bigger bucket, which was standing in a water trough with a sort of hose attachment running water down the sides. 'This cools the milk; then it goes in the container to be collected. Are you glad you finally made it?'

'I'm fascinated. Never seen anything like it. Do the cows always just stand there?'

'They're on their best behaviour because you're here. But if they're in a bad mood or bulling, it can be interesting. But they are held on a neck chain. Come and watch the process through again and then you can have a go!'

Mollie stood and watched, suddenly realising she was really preparing herself to have a go. There was soon one cow left, and Chris turned to her as if reading her mind and cocked an eyebrow.

'Do you really think I can?'

'I'll watch your every move. Now this is Clara, and she's always last, as she's a patient soul. Give her a stroke, talk to her and introduce yourself. Your touch will be different to mine.'

Mollie did as she was bid, rubbing Clara's neck with the firm touch she would give a horse. Clara swung her head, breathed a dragon's breath and a pointed tongue tipped out of her mouth to investigate. She raised her head, and her third eyelids came over her eyes as she tried to look forwards. Then the tongue came right out, and Mollie had her first experience of the roughness of a cow's tongue. It rasped her skin but didn't damage. It seemed Mollie was approved as Clara swung her head back to her mound of hay.

'Right, now get a cloth from the bucket and wipe her teats gently. She's quite a clean cow, not like Sam over there, but it's better for the milk.'

Molly did so cautiously, finding the teats firmer than she had expected. Copying Chris, she threw the cloth by the bucket and picked up the milking equipment. She was fine until the last teat, where she nearly sucked up some hay, but the clicker got going and the milk gushed.

'Now, while she is going, you need to take off the last few drips of milk from the udder of Sam. Close your fingers around the teat and squeeze down; there's only a little there.' Using her stool, Mollie crouched and gingerly grabbed and squeezed. To her surprise, milk came out easily, but stopped after a couple of goes. The others were the same. Taking the cream, she rubbed that in and stood up.

'Do you hear the change?' The squelching was getting louder. She quickly went back to Clara and released the line, inwardly rejoicing that she didn't drop the cluster and made it to the bench.

'Wow, that was amazing!'

'You're not finished yet, you must strip Clara.'

In her haste, Mollie nearly dropped the tin, but

managed. When she got back, Chris was tipping the milk into the delivery churn.

'You might find this a bit heavy, but we can work around this, I think!'

'You really want me to do this?' Mollie was a bit worried.

'It would be really nice to have the occasional lie in and a weekend off, and yes, it was part of the deal, wasn't it?'

'I know, but trusting me, such a beginner, with the cows.'

'I would never be that far away at first.'

'I really enjoyed it, so, yes, I can see me doing it.'

Mollie found herself stroking Clara. 'Introduce me to the rest of the ladies.' So far, Mollie had only seen the herd from the kitchen window. It was like a light had switched on with Chris. He went to the head of the line and as he untied the neck chains and the tail strings, he was off. Mollie was itching to ask what the strings were for, but she couldn't get a word in edgeways.

'There are two more outside, Ziggy and Queenie; they are dry; they should calf next month. This is Imogen. She can be tetchy if she isn't first in line. Did I say, they're all Jersey cross, with either Hereford for beef or Friesian for milk. This apparently is why she has these stripes. Some of the crosses look just like Herefords. I pick and mix with the bulls, but don't take the mixture too far away from the Jersey. I quite like looking at the family trees: I keep them written down and looking through the AI catalogue passes time in the winter.' Most of this was double Dutch to Mollie. It seemed that Chris needed to get out a bit more. Imogen mooched out. 'This is Katharina, gracious lady, but maybe the most stupid of the lot. After her is Patience, because we needed a lot with her when she was a calf. Then Sam, she's a pure Jersey. Actually, I was one short. Then Grumpy here, who is the real cow of the lot, but she let you wipe her teats without an introduction, so I think you'll be all right with her.'

'Maybe it's because I work with horses; I can touch animals and feel with them. They are just so different to horses, sort of dreamy.'

'You mean dozy! Well, they're still more of a herd animal, I suppose, not so high up the domestic order. If you treat them right, they're lovely. No whacking with sticks here.'

The cows were slowly making their way out, Clara and Grumpy tussling in the door way. Mollie picked up her jumper. She knew now why Chris was only in a T-shirt.

'I'm lucky here; I have enough land that I just let them roam at will all year. It's only while Keith is here that I keep them separate from the horses. That reminds me, he's due to go tomorrow. She's dragged it out until the end of my patience, there haven't been any mares for weeks. Maybe you might want to make yourself scarce when she arrives?'

'Too flipping true, I'll go shopping, but you'll

need to keep the dogs in.'

'No problem. Now we must clear up. You get that broom and sweep all the poop to the drain at the end, and I'll follow with the hose. Andy will collect the milk later this morning.'

'Andy?'

'Did I not tell you? I suppose we've been so busy moving you in! He's tenant farmer on the other side of the estate, and he's just set up cheese making. I sold him all the gear from the dairy, and he now takes my nice, high fat milk to improve his Friesian, weak as water stuff!'

'So why do you keep them if you aren't making cheese anymore?'

'Milk sales make a good income, along with all the subsidies. I get along okay. It helps owning the place, not being a tenant farmer. I have just been ticking over here for the past few years, as I told you. I don't really want to be a farmer, but I haven't quite worked out how and what is the alternative.'

'How come you own the place? The estate is as tight as a drum with the land.'

'Maybe things were different in the past, but we've had this place, I think, since the big fire. Dad used to tell me tales about great, great something, something Grandfather helping with clearing the old house out, he was first on the scene.'

'How on earth do you remember things from so long ago?'

'Family tales passed down on long winter nights by the fire!'

He put the hose away and then showed Mollie how to strip, disinfect, wash through, and hang the equipment to dry. Chris laughed when he saw Mollie's pale face. 'Breakfast? It's been quite a long session!'

Mollie suddenly realised that it was now light, another sunshiny day in prospect. The cool fresh air was a relief after the smell of the cows. A wave of tiredness ran over her, her watch said 6.30, what time had she got up?

'5 o'clock.' Chris read her mind.

'Does it have to be so early?'

'Well, the payback is evening milking is now at 5ish, so the evening is free.'

They walked into the kitchen to find the dogs were now up, wanting out and breakfast at the same time. Cereal and toast were now a familiar routine, then Chris was off to the sitting room. 'I'm just going to watch the news headlines. Then we'll have to put the hay ready for tonight; it saves time. I'll put the delivery out.' Mollie grinned at his retreating back. For someone who had only had a small set in the kitchen, he had taken to her smart TV like a duck to water, of course, after she had paid for the internet to be installed. She stretched, got up, put the breakfast things away and went to join him.

EIGHT

Early afternoon had Mollie collecting the dogs and setting off for a long walk. Chris had instructions to call her once Liz was gone. She strode up through the fields feeling happy. She knew her way quite well around the fields now, but Chris had told her of a viewpoint that looked down over Hazeley manor and as far as the sea. The day was crisp and clear, so she had her camera with her, too. There were so many paths she didn't know, but now she was free from the stables, she had time on her hands. Well, for a while anyway, but now it was such a luxury to be out and about during the day and not under someone's command.

The dogs were actually behaving themselves and didn't disappear hunting for rabbits, which was heaven. She found the clump of beech trees and followed the path through, then, in surprise, stood there drinking it all in. Below her was the red brick Victorian manor. She could see the stables, the outdoor school, even some horses out in the paddock. Then the village, her old house, where she could see a removal van parked outside. She didn't linger. The church, the shop and the rolling fields of the estate. Then the river Itchen, wending its slow way to the sea at Southampton, and in the far distance, Thorn's Beach and the beginning of the New Forest. She got her camera and snapped distance, landscape, panorama and zoom until she could do no more. It was ominously quiet; where were the dogs? She turned around in a sudden panic and jumped out of her skin as she saw a woman about her own age with long blonde hair sat on the bench, smiling a broad grin at her. The dogs were talking to two new arrivals, a slender black dog and a rather moth eaten brown one.

'I didn't want to spoil your photo moment! It's a stunning view, isn't it?'

'I lived in the village for two years and never knew about this. It's gob smacking. Hi, I'm Mollie.'

'I'm Joanna. I live in that old place down there.'

'Oh, right, the lady of The Manor!' Mollie was playing for time. This was Liz's boss, who owned the stables.

'I've seen you out and about with the horses, and yes, I know about you and Liz!' She was still smiling, but Mollie's stomach was turning.

'Is that a good or a bad thing?'

'I didn't employ Liz; it was my evil stepmother, Diane, who's actually younger than me. None of my business, really. It's very complicated. She was my best friend who married my dad. She's off somewhere hot and sunny doing native stuff with my dad! Don't look so worried. Tell me about your dogs. Rex we already know quite well.'

Mollie sat down with relief and told her all about Ratty and Mutantmutt, and soon they were giggling about the story of how Mutantmutt had knocked James over. The dogs were playing and sitting in various modes.

'I used to have two black dogs, but Jack was drowned. My now husband found me Tim, who was abused. Even after all this time, his ears haven't really healed. Guy trains dogs and helps me with the business.'

Mollie was wondering why she was getting all this information.

'Okay, I can guess what you're thinking. You have been a bit set up. I bumped into Chris in the shop the other day; he was the one who told me about you and Liz, and that you might need a part-time job and you, er, were heading this way this afternoon.'

'I'll kill him.'

'Oh, don't do that, you might make a mess, and what would the cows do?'

That forced a grin from Mollie. 'I'm not in desperate need for the immediate future, but I will need something. I was milking for the first time today. That's going to be a job that needs getting used to with the early starts. I was only just congratulating myself on my freedom as I walked up here. Should have guessed it would be short lived! What exactly do you want?'

Joanna was off. 'You're in for it now! Well, it's all mostly because we're pregnant, and the baby is due not long before Christmas. I run a business with two guys, collecting and organising archive documents for people who have sent them to an archive office, but have had them rejected or want to keep them for themselves. We then help them with running them if they put them onto one of the websites. We have an archive here of family documents, which I look after. Jan and Harry do a lot of travelling when it is onsite, but some of it comes back here, and sometimes people just want someone else to do it. Hence, we now have a growing storage problem and these need organising.'

Mollie couldn't see how she could possibly do this, as she had no experience apart from horses and dogs.

'I'm being really sick in the mornings and I just need someone to help with what I can't deal with. Dog walking, cleaning, humping boxes, maybe answering some routine emails, taking phone messages ... possibly cooking.'

'I'm no cook, but I could help with the other stuff,' said Mollie with a sense of relief. 'Like one of those girl Friday type things?'

'You've got it! The hours are fairly flexible, and I would only need about fifteen hours a week to start with; you'd be properly employed through the business. Of course, the dogs can come as well. I won't tell Guy about Mutantmutt's pole axing technique!'

They both sat for a moment in silence. Mollie felt quite peaceful after her original irritation.

'Well, I don't see why not; we could give it a try,'

she smiled.

'That's wonderful! But there is one thing we need to do to seal it. Walk with me down to the house for a coffee? If you want to avoid Liz, we'll take the back lane and come in through the garden. You can drive in that way, too, rather than past the stables.'

Mollie was grateful for the understanding. But just what had Chris told Joanna? They made their way down the hill with companionable chatter about the village and the show, each feeling their way with the other. Soon, they arrived at the back of the house. Mollie looked up at the tall building with its green shutters that matched the stables.

'We've just walked through the footings of the original manor that burnt down. My rellies built this as a smaller replacement. The original was huge; we mapped out a plan last year.'

'Chris was only telling me today that his family got the farm just after the fire. One of his grandfathers had helped in rescuing the furniture and stuff. Amazing what gets passed down the generations.'

'I never knew that. I must talk to him about that sometime; I've never really thought about why they owned the place. Now here is the final test. When I was going through some stuff, Challenger, who I used to show jump, was acutely aware of what I was really feeling inside, even if I wasn't. In fact, he tried to kick my head in when he first returned here.'

Grazing in a small paddock was a large bay thoroughbred horse with a small Shetland beside him. Challenger turned and walked with a long but stiff stride towards them. His back was saggy and his hip bones showed. They went through the gate to greet the horses.

'How old is he?' asked Mollie, going up to the old boy and stroking his nose. He was sniffing her.

'He's in his thirties.' Challenger then blew his nose over Mollie's jacket and looked away, bored. 'Does this mean I...ouch!' The Shetland, not wanting to be missed out, was head butting her. She gave him a scratch too; Joanna now stroking Challenger.

'I have missed the contact with horses,' said Mollie wistfully, 'but I think cows might be just as good for a cuddle when I get to know them.' At this point, the horses turned as if disgusted and walked away.

'You certainly passed the test on both scores, but then you insulted them by comparing them to cows!!!' Joanna laughed. 'We rescued Bill when the riding centre he belonged to closed. He was with us when we did some therapy and we felt we owed him.'

'Therapy?'

'That's another story! Let's go in. Come on, dogs!'

The house was an eye-opener for Mollie, as Joanna guided her through the hall to the kitchen at the back.

'Guy and I have spent a lot of time trying to

restore this to some of its Victorian glory. I used to live in the servants' wing and as we found the kitchen too small on the main side, we still use mine. They swung through an ornate baize door and into a homely kitchen.

'We gave up with the renovations here, as we liked it too much! Tea or coffee?'

'Coffee, please. Just look at the dogs. They could have been friends for years!' All five were jostling for a place on a large, rumpled sofa that was obviously a dog domain.

'Seems like they've decided you get the job, too.'

'Looks like I don't have a choice, doesn't' it?' laughed Mollie. 'Tell me more about my duties and where things are!'

The two spent a comfortable couple of hours looking at the archive, the office, the kitchen, and the cleaning cupboard, until Mollie was really quite happy she could do this. She was drawn to Joanna, but couldn't put her finger on what it was. Maybe it was that there seemed to be no side to her, a genuine person. They parted through the back garden, where the dogs could be safe while she worked, and she made her way back up the hill feeling for the first time in quite a while that things might just work out after all.

Chris watched Liz drive away, with Keith shouting his annoyance from inside the trailer. It had been a slightly tense meeting, but Liz made no reference to Mollie. Hopefully, with the Land Rover hidden behind the dairy and the dogs out of the way, there was no way to link her to him. But in this village, everyone knew everyone's business. But at least he wouldn't have any dealing with Liz for the near future. She had actually paid him for the grazing, too, which was a surprise. He turned and went back into the house. As he reached for the remote control of the TV, he was suddenly aware of all the clutter that was now strewn around the place. Mollie's cups, books, magazines, and discarded clothes. How could one person strew so much about? He gathered up a few bits and pieces to make a place for himself on the sofa but couldn't settle.

He now needed a cup of coffee, too. In the kitchen, above the aga was the dryer, now full of Mollie's underwear. Intrigued because his mother had been such a private person, he reached up and pulled some of them down. How could something so small be comfortable? Didn't it ride up as you walked? He couldn't imagine having such a chest that it filled these cups. He looked around him as if Mollie might come bursting in and catch him in the act. But Joanna had promised to ring when she left in case Liz was still around. It was no good; he ran up to the bathroom and tried them on. The briefs were surprisingly comfortable, but he didn't have much to pack into them. The bra just looked daft. He was just reaching for some loo roll to pad them out when he heard Mollie calling to the dogs across the yard. He slammed the door shut and put his clothes back on over the underwear and went down to meet her. Funny, they didn't seem to ride up…

NINE

Milking for the second time was much easier for Mollie. She was on a high about meeting Joanna, having completely forgiven a very sheepish Chris for his duplicity. Whether she would feel the same when she started was another thing altogether. She found she was already becoming familiar with the rhythm of the work and the company of the cows. It was less stressful than having to tack up, muck out, feed, clean tack. The simplicity of the job as a joy. The cows seemed to like her, too; they didn't try to kick or be bolshy. She scratched their heads behind where the horns had been and along their necks. Chris stood back and let her work, only venturing a comment when she could improve something. They then washed up in companionable banter.

Afterwards, he dropped a bombshell. 'I'm going to have my first lie in for five years tomorrow morning. You're doing so well!'

'Are you sure?'

'I'm that tired. As long as you get the collection ready in time, you can take as long as you like!'

Mollie was silent for a moment. Both terrifying and exciting.

'There is only one thing left to do. We must go

and check the two down calvers who are lurking around outside. Both are due in the next couple of weeks.'

'What do you do with the calves? I haven't seen any around the place?'

'The bulls and some heifers go off to a rearing farm the other side of the village, and if I need a replacement, she stays.'

'With mum?'

'No, after three days we separate them because we want the milk. Can't have milk and calf, too.'

'Why not?'

'Well, it's standard farming practise.'

'Doesn't mean it's right. You're not a big producer. Would a few gallons down make any difference?' Mollie could feel something like panic rising within her. She didn't understand it but voiced it. 'That seems so unfair, like some form of torture, to let them love their babies for a few days and then to snatch them away; that's almost more than separating them at birth.'

'I've never really thought about it… but to please you, I will! It doesn't really matter to me that much.' He smiled roguishly and they went through the muddy yard to the field. The two cows of the stripy variant were under some trees. Chris checked their teats and then was prodding around the base of their tails.

'The muscles relax here and that's a sure sign. Ziggy here has suddenly got a lot of milk. She's bagged up, so we'll bring her in, though I suppose the other will insist on coming, too.'

He turned and gave each cow a tap on the bum and hushed them on. Both turned and walked away from him in the wrong direction.

'Quick, before they get into the upper field; run and get in front.'

Mollie legged it through the mud and managed to turn the two, who gave in without much of a fuss and went into the barn adjoining the milking parlour. Chris put them into a small enclosure, deep bedded, ready for calving.

'We got off lightly with these two. They're really good at the disappearing act! Um...tomorrow is my birthday. My uncle and aunt always turn up in the evening. Will you be around?'

'Yes, of course; do we do cake and party like mad?'

'No, they're both in their 80s. I get a cake from the local bakery and they drink a glass of sherry, then go.'

'Then down to the pub afterwards?

'Not my sort of thing, but maybe we'll get a takeaway?'

'My, you do have a quiet life!'

'Not a great socialiser, as you know!'

Mollie was thinking frantically about what to get him, then had a brainwave. She had seen him eying up her laptop. He was unbelievably computer ignorant, never having bothered with it before, but she could tell he would like one, especially the way he had taken to her TV. Could anyone really be so cut off from the world these days? They shut off the lights in the barn and went back into the house. Mollie then made her excuses, as she now needed to get her laptop out and order Chris his. With her membership, she knew that it would arrive the next day. Hugging the excitement to herself that night, she set the alarm for that ridiculously early hour and tried to get to sleep.

All this milking lark seemed like just one stupid idea when it rang the next morning, with no gentle awakening from Chris's clogs. Even the dogs weren't amused and didn't even cock an ear as she stumbled around the room. Still, the early morning light was like a tonic and Mollie perked up as she crossed the yard. The cows were waiting outside and came eagerly to the heaps of hay that she had set out the previous evening. Chains on necks, Mollie collected the milking equipment and switched everything on.

There was so much to remember, and without Chris, she suddenly didn't feel so sure. She took Sam as her first and all seemed to go well until she went to get the cleaning cloths. Sam turned and looked, then lifted one hoof and carefully put it on the bucket and cluster, turning it on its side causing a huge, nasty sucking sound. This was then an excuse to sidle about and look alarmed. Without thinking, Mollie went into horse mode, 'Now just stop messing about and behave yourself,' and she slapped Sam on the bum. Sam stopped and looked down as Mollie righted the bucket, then swung her coup de grace. Mollie hadn't understood what the strings were for, but she now did as a stinking, sodden tail caught her accurately right in the eye. This time she really did yell, as it stung so much. Sam went back to her hay as if she'd done nothing. Mopping her stinging eye, Mollie tied the tails of all the cows and then realised the squeak was now squawking and she hadn't cleaned Katharina's teats, which were liberally covered in dung. How did they manage that when they were all out in a field?

No, she wasn't going to panic. She took a deep breath and removed the teat and went and emptied the bucket. There was no time limit, no Liz shouting orders, so if it took longer than usual, there was no problem. That didn't mean that each cow didn't try some sort of trick on her. Sidestepping, shoving, farting, trying to wee and poo on her with specially saved runny dung, taking ages to let the milk down when she tried to strip the teats and, best of all, kicking one sucker off just as she put another on. Each time though, she treated them as horses, with firmness and a stroke when they behaved.

As she finished Grumpy, who was actually the best behaved, she realised that the sun was well and truly up, and Chris was watching her with an amused grin from the door.

'How many of their tricks did they try?'

'You mean the sidestepping, poo flinging, dancing ones? All of them, I guess.' Mollie suddenly felt exhausted. 'It's just like when you have a new horse; they push all the boundaries to see what they can get away with!'

'And who won?'

'Oh, definitely me; I even have enough milk for the cats. Only odd thing is Grumpy's milk seemed thicker than the others.'

'She's prone to mastitis; was her final milk, ok?'

'Seemed to be.'

'I'll check her this evening, then if there is a problem, I can introduce you to the joys of cow medicating! I only slept in an hour, but I feel completely refreshed. Come and have some breakfast with me.'

They let the cows out and checked the calvers, who were just munching and looking fat. Chris gave Ziggy the benefit of doubt and let them both out, too.

To her surprise, Mollie found Chris had cooked breakfast, and she was really hungry. 'Happy Birthday, Chris...just how old are you?'

'I hate to admit it, but twenty five.'

'Oh, ancient, I'm twenty three! I've got you a pressie ordered. It should arrive by lunchtime, so you'll have to contain your excitement until then!' She saw that despite her news, he suddenly looked sad.

'They never match up to those childhood birthdays, do they?' He smiled wanly.

'Not for me; I hated them. I used to have these awful parties my parents would organise, and I never had any say as to who was invited. It was mostly kids of their friends and the wealthier ones in my class. I hated every minute. Now they're better. I can just go down to the pub, or actually just buy me a cake and not really celebrate them at all. I prefer them now. '

'My parents didn't like parties. A couple of times, the kids from the next farm would come to tea, and that was about it. It got worse as I got older. I wanted to go out to places like McDonalds, but they would never go.'

'Your folks seem quite the opposite to my two ravers then. They were never at home.'

'Lucky you; my two were claustrophobic at best. Highly protective, they made my childhood seem like there was always something to protect me from, but they wouldn't say what. I only went to the village school for a couple of years; then they taught me at home.'

'That sounds awful. We seem to have had the worst of both worlds.'

With incredible timing before the conversation could get any more difficult, a delivery van came screaming into the yard, setting all the dogs off into a fury of barking. Mollie rushed out and waded through them with various curses and took the parcel through the window. She sped back with great glee.

'Happy Birthday! I've seen you coveting my laptop, so I got you one! We can get it set up and you can play as much as you like.'

'Wow, thanks, but what will I do with it exactly?

'Well, look up bulls for the cows. More about milk quotas?' Mollie realised that he couldn't look for old school friends at all. 'We can set you up with a Facebook account, and you can talk to the other breeders and farmers in the area. What about photos?'

'Ah, yes, I am actually digital on that!'

'And you might look at your Bible school you went to. They might do online classes now. And what about the church thing you do with Joanna? didn't you say they use films and stuff?'

Chris brightened at this idea and they both fell to with the unpacking. It was the usual problem with wires and cables and programmes, but a couple of hours later, Chris was set up with various websites to look at. Even if he had refused Facebook, he had some shopping pages, mostly for dairy equipment, the bible school, the church network and she showed him how to do searches and send emails. Mollie was exhausted, but Chris cleared a table in the study by just sweeping all the old documents from his father's accounts onto the floor, and she left him cursing and swearing as he found his way around a new world.

He had said that his rellies would have cake and tea when they arrived, so she had a go at tidying the kitchen. Where a lot of it wasn't her stuff, she wasn't too happy at starting to move things around. Then she saw some of the mail and catalogues dated back over five years, so like

Chris, she swept the lot into a box and shoved it into a cupboard. She had enjoyed the cleaning of the holiday house, so she really got into giving the room a going over. It soon looked like something from a countryside calendar. Chris was so absorbed that she took the Land Rover and went to collect his cake. She took the dogs for a walk, and he was still ensconced. Suddenly, Mollie found herself at a loose end, so she tidied her room, even ran the hoover over the dog- haired house. It was no good. She had to disturb him; they had to get on with milking. For once she found it difficult to burst in on him. He was bent over the table in a trance and didn't hear her at first, then jumped out of his skin, turning almost as if to divert her from seeing the screen. His eyes were red from staring.

'Good grief Chris, you really look like you've been burning the midnight oil! Go and look in the mirror.'

'How do I turn it off?'

'On the side menu, it'll prompt you.'

He did so with his new-found skills. 'Thanks so much. I've had a lot of fun with my new toy. Don't know why I've not bothered before. Do you know there's another farmer near Basingstoke who is running the same crosses with his cows? I even sent him an email!'

'But now we need to milk!'

'Oh, right, yes, and aunt and uncle will be here. Oh, no, the cake!' It was like he was swimming to the surface.

'It's all under control! I've collected it and I've even cleaned the kitchen in your honour. By the way, have you seen a red underwear set? I was sure it was on the dryer?'

TEN

Milking was quickly done with the two of them working as a team, and they were ready and not smelling so much of cow when an old mini drew into the yard. Chris went out while Mollie watched with great interest. There were no big hugs, but a cheerfulness; then he led the two indoors.

'This is Mollie, who has come to help with the cows.' Chris shot her a warning look. Compromise land again. Mollie shook hands formally. Chris's uncle was tall with a stoop, but with the same blonde colouring that she guessed must run in the family. His blue eyes twinkled, and she had the sudden feeling that he was reading what wasn't there. The aunt was a picture perfect aunt, plump with tightly curled hair, glasses and the same merriness about her.

'So nice to meet you. Have you been here long?'

'Just a couple of months. Are you all right with dogs? My two are shut in the outhouse, but they're friendly.'

'We love dogs, but can't have one in the flat, which is such a shame. Do let them in. We can't see Rex; is he with them?'

Mollie responded by letting the dogs out, who found themselves meeting a flurry of cuddles and treats.

'I don't think you come here to see me at all,' Chris pretended to grumble, and they all went into the kitchen, dogs fussing and twirling.

'Get that tea on lad… I see someone has been cleaning!' Mollie received approving looks.

'All in your honour, of course!' Chris said from tea making.

'And chocolate cake.' There weren't any candles though. The discussion got into the cows and fields. Mollie sat and listened. Aunt, who now insisted she should be called Jane, smiled at her through the conversation as they sipped tea and ate cake. The conversation turned to computers.

'I'm now the proud owner of a laptop; Mollie gave me it!'

'We said last year that you should get one! We'll send you a friend request when we get back tonight. It'll be so much easier to keep in touch. Are you on Instagram?'

Mollie was bowled over by their computer savviness, and then Henry insisted he go and help Chris set up his Facebook account, leaving the two women alone.

'So!' Jane smiled. 'What's the actual story about you being here?'

Mollie knew she wouldn't get away with anything with that bright stare, so she told her the whole story.

'Sounds like you've had a hard time,' said Jane when she had finished. 'But it will do the world of good for Chris to have some company.'

'He was telling me that he was taught by his parents. That's unusual, isn't it?' Mollie couldn't resist getting the dirt on Chris. Jane looked a little phased, then leant forward conspiratorially.

'Well, he was a very late and unexpected child. Marion was 45 when he was born, but she had an easy delivery – she was Henry's sister, of course. He looked lovely to us. Well, we went to visit them in hospital, and as we arrived, we found she was in a private room with a load of doctors inside, and we had to wait. When they came out, they were all arguing about something, and then we went in. Marion and Tony were very po-faced but said that she was very tired, and could we visit at home? What could we do? We left the gifts and visited them the following week. She was fine then, but I'm sure there was something up. But she would never speak about it.

They were always very protective of him. Only child, I suppose. He went to the local playschool, the creche at church and did one year at the local primary school. Then suddenly, they took him out and began teaching him themselves. Marion threw herself into it; she took all sorts of evening classes, so she could do it right. When Chris took his GCSEs, she took some, too. He went to cubs and later the Young Farmers, but he must just be a loner. He's never had real friends. Always working on the farm with his dad. It's a shame they stopped breeding the ponies; Tony was sort of sad when they went… There were always kids about the place mucking about with the horses, but Chris sort of kept his distance,' she sighed. 'Then Chris opted to go to Bible school, and then came the accident, so he came home. Been on his own for the past five years, so you can see, we're so thrilled to find you here!' Jane sat back, but before Mollie could pelt her with questions, the men returned. Chris looked at her and raised an eyebrow, and Mollie felt herself blushing. Fortunately, the conversation was quickly directed into what and who they had seen on Facebook, and Mollie made herself busy with pouring more tea.

Before long, the two were making their goodbyes and promising to come and visit more often and they drove away in the gathering dusk.

'What was she saying then?'

'Just about how you had a very solitary childhood, and she's pleased that I'm here.'

'Everyone goes on about that, but I'm not unique. Gary, over the other side of the estate is farming on his own. I don't know why everyone wants to match make for me!'

'It's only natural, Chris. You haven't had an easy time of it, have you?'

'Seems just like life to me; just take the rough with the smooth.'

'Compromise living, Chris! They've gone away with many happy ideas about us in their heads. Let them be. They're really the most remarkable pair; at least they turn up for your birthday, not like my lot!'

'You're right. Just being sensitive, I suppose. You start work on Monday. How about us taking the mares out for a ride tomorrow? They've not been ridden all summer, and I can show you more of the estate. We could take the dogs and something to eat.'

'And milking?'

'If we don't hang around afterwards, we'll have loads of time.'

'That sounds great, let's do!'

The two mares were easily caught the following morning, and after they tied them up in the yard, Mollie and Chris went into the old tack room. Mollie was astonished. Inside hung at least ten sets of tack and all sorts of other equipment, all signs of a great deal of professional horse activity. Rosettes, now dusty and drooping, were mixed with photos of Chris and his parents at various shows. Mollie, of course, had to snoop.

'Wow, your parents had quite a success with them. You won the County trophy? On a cob? Boy, she must have had a jump on her!'

'That was Tinker; she was incredible. After that, we put her to stud, and she had three foals, all of which were jumpers too.'

'So what happened? Jane said you had at least two stallions. It must have been quite a thing!'

'It was Dad when I said I didn't want to run the farm and the stud. He said he wasn't going to sweat any more building it up for me; he was going to sell up and retire. And he did. He and Mum were going to go on a cruise after I left.' Chris sat down, suddenly defeated. 'If I hadn't been so set on Bible school, they still would be here.'

'There are always two sides to a story', thought Mollie, but said nothing about it. 'You're still beating yourself up about that?'

'But of course; it was cause and effect.'

'All right, but the cause of the accident wasn't ever sorted out, was it? There was maybe some random factor. If the car was faulty, maybe it would have happened the next day. Then you would still grieve, but not so responsible.'

'I see your point. When I pray about it, I know and feel I'm forgiven, but it always comes back. I can't shake it off.'

'Why do you need God to forgive you? It was just circumstances. Unless you think it was God that did this?'

'No, of course, he didn't do it.'

'Why shouldn't He if He has something He needs to teach us? Make us suffer so we become more like Him?'

'Who told you that nonsense?'

'The priest from our church. I was brought up a Catholic. It was always God needs to squash you; you must repent, pay for all your sins that you do. Even breathing seems like a sin.' Mollie was aware of the bitterness in her voice. 'When I was about 10, I did all my repenting. Did confession every day for a week. Prayed the rosary. I reckoned I had a bit of credit with God. So, I asked Him to make my parents like me. Didn't work. The next day I was told I had to stay in school for the Easter holidays if I couldn't find a friend to stay with, as my parents were off on holiday. No, God doesn't exist as far as I'm concerned.'

'That's not the God I know.'

'It seems exactly like the one I knew, seeing as you're still in a mess after five years!' Mollie knew from his face she had overstepped some sort of mark. 'Sorry, maybe we need to agree to differ on this one?'

'Yeah, we're poles apart and we have to get along. That flipping word again?'

Mollie nodded, and they grinned. Chris pointed her to some tack, and they went out and groomed the ponies. They were full of dirt from their lazy summer; the dust and dirt flew. The sun was shining and suddenly all seemed good to Mollie as they swung aboard and called the dogs to follow. It was the first time she had ridden for herself in a long time; no riders to check, no need to keep her ears peeled for traffic and screams. She could relax. She patted Dixie's thick neck and jogged along.

'Why did you keep these two, then?'

'Sentiment, I suppose. These were two foals that were left about the place when I went. I had broken them in myself, but never got around to selling them, so it seemed a good idea to breed from them. They've both got good lines, but I'm not sure how it will work out with the foals, as Keith is a Welsh section D, not an ordinary cob like these. Hey, look, there's Keith's bit on the side!'

They were passing the field with the shire mare in it. She came rushing up to the fence to have a chat.

'Is she in foal?'

'They think so. I wonder what colour it will be? She's black and he's palomino.'

'Could be a piebald, with short legs, big feet, a short back and a small Araby head!'

Chris snorted. 'Just so long as it's not just like Keith.'

'Did Liz have anything to say when she came around?'

'No, she was her usual blunt self; seemed in a hurry to go and not give instructions. Not at all like herself; she paid me in cash.'

Mollie felt the drag of those days coming back to her. No more, she was free in all ways.

'Come on Chris, let's give it some welly!'

He turned and grinned at her, put his heels on his mount, and they took off up the hill. Dixie was short striding, but fast. A little wary, Mollie concentrated hard, but there seemed no side to the mare. She just wanted to keep up with her buddy, so Mollie relaxed, to enjoy the air blasting past her face, not having to keep checking behind, simply the thrill of a good gallop. But the mares weren't fit and soon they began to puff, and they slowed to a walk. Mutantmutt, Ratty and Rex, equally puffy, caught up, and all stood to catch their breaths.

'You forget what fun it is when you have to take kids out all the time.'

'Just enjoy it Mollie; stop thinking!' laughed Chris and picked up his reins. They went on along the track in quiet enjoyment. The occasional snort from the horses, hoof thuds and quietness. Mollie let herself at last completely relax and enjoy the rhythm. A couple of trots and canters later, they came to a clearing in some woods. It was obviously used as a picnic place, so they put the halters on the horses and tied them to the trees so they could graze. Chris opened his backpack and they feasted on birthday cake, crisps and thermos tea. The dogs had chews, but they didn't last long. They all lay in the sun, except for Mutantmutt, who had to collect sticks and drop them at feet to be thrown, but eventually she came, too, and sprawled in the sunshine.

'That was wonderful! If my mother was here, we would have had to have a picnic basket, wine and blankets!'

'Mollie!' said Chris in a warning voice.

'Oh, I know, I know... did you come here as a kid?'

'Yeah, we used to have a ring of jumps at the edge of the wood and go belting around.'

'Did you add me as a friend on Facebook?'

'Yes, Mollie!'

'Can I ride Dixie a little bit more until she's too fat? I haven't ridden a pony for such a long time. She's so free and willing.'

'Don't see why not. Why don't you try Pixie here on the way back?'

'Pixie and Dixie? Good grief, you must have spent a lot of time watching cartoons when you were a kid!'

'I guess I did. What was your favourite?'

'When I got a chance, I watched Friends, not so many cartoons.'

'What, not even Power Rangers or He-man?'

'Na, not my style. Anyway, I'm sure He-Man was gay!'

At which point, Chris threw a cup at Mollie for insulting his hero. They bridled the ponies again and went to look for the old jumps. To their joy, someone had kept them mended, so with whoops of glee, they hurtled around. That was until Pixie decided that, as a pregnant lady, she was out of breath and stopped. Chris shot over her shoulder, and as Dixie stopped on Pixie's rump, Mollie shot over her shoulder, and they both lay on the ground with fits of giggles, quite unhurt. Eventually, they sat up and rubbed bits of wood and leaves off themselves.

'I haven't had such fun for years,' said Mollie extracting a leaf from her mouth.

'Me, too; maybe we need a second childhood!' They got up, rode home more gently through the autumnal lanes, chatting and bickering and deciding whether to buy an Xbox.

James was pacing up and down outside Ava's office, once again waiting for her summons. He really didn't think that it would be as bad as last time. He'd been a good boy, had jumped through all the hurdles and hoops expected of him in rehab and the anonymous, the 'getting off things ` groups. He now had to attend. Glowing reports from them all. He had to admit as well, it was nice to be thinking clearly, remembering things and, above all finding his muse to write again. After all, he needed the cash. The couple of articles he'd managed to get printed about his return to writing and life had brought a little income, but not enough. He really had to get that painting back, and now he knew where it was. He was ushered in.

'Lovely, James!' she was all smiles. 'Just what the public wants and with the hot political theme, it'll fly off the shelves.' So, reading all those newspapers to ease the boredom had paid off. 'We'll publish for the Christmas market, so keep your diary free from the beginning of November!'

'Any chance of some, er, advance royalties? I've had to pay for all these therapies. They're not cheap.'

'Well, we will have the film rights money from the last book soon, so I will send that as soon as it arrives.' James perked up; he had forgotten about that. They shook hands amicably and he was off. After a few days rest he would have to take himself to Hampshire again, but in the meantime, his favourite little tin was full, and he was off to party.

ELEVEN

Chris watched Mollie drive away for her first day at the Manor. She had been a bundle of nerves with the cows until, in the end, he had sent her up the field to check on the calvers. He turned with glee. Now he was free of interruption and questions to do the searches on the laptop he was longing to do. His Bible stared at him. Was what he was doing wrong? He sat and looked at it mesmerised. Mollie being in the house had caused all he held right and dear to be questioned.

All his life he had accepted things as the norm, and suddenly there was the possibility that they weren't. His parents, he suddenly saw as overprotective, rather than just being normal. He could remember that at playschool and the first couple of years in the village school, nothing struck him as terrible or odd there. Then he was suddenly taught at home. What had his parents said? That they thought the standard was too low? He hadn't minded. He still went to cubs and scouts and later the Young Farmers. He'd played with the other farmers' kids who came to ride the ponies when there was the opportunity. But mostly, he'd been around the farm with his parents, with the ponies and cows. They'd done lots of showing, too.

Wasn't that usual for a farming family? He still drank with the lads in the pub on occasion, but since his parents' deaths, less and less, especially as the others were all marrying or moving away.

So why did he have this sense of separateness? Was it because he had never bothered with girlfriends? Just the occasional dance and snog at a dance that had left him feeling untouched? Why did he hate it so much when the riding club girls tried to get him to join them? He felt like an island. Did people see something in him that they didn't like? Mollie had made it clear she didn't want any sort of relationship except buddies, and that was the best thing in five years. Yesterday had been a blast. But having someone his age in the house and all her girly things were shaking something up in him, but he didn't know what, except it was something sexual.

His parents had told him the facts of life as if he hadn't guessed it from having stallions about the place, but it hadn't touched him. The Bible school, his years in the church youth groups, and his parent's beliefs had set something in stone within him. Bible school seemed the way to go, as he really didn't want to spend his life working with horses and cows. It was the only option he had seen, but it had felt right. And now he was trapped. He could sell the farm, but the place had his heart, and he knew that whatever he would do, he would need to be able to come back here.

Sighing, 'Sorry God, I must find this out for

myself. What this storm is that's growing in me. I would not do anything to displease you, but I must find out and this seems the best way.' He clicked onto the Internet. First of all, he searched through the gay websites for men and women. Then the transgender, then the bisexual. Some bits he found interesting, some he could sort of identify with, some revolted him. All attracted him in some sort of way. He pushed his chair back from the computer. He had really thought he would have some quick answers, but no. What was wrong with him then? Would he really have to go to the doctor's to talk about his messed up feelings? It seemed he wasn't attracted to men or women, just a little of both. Surely it had to be one or both? Nothing seemed to interest him, except that day when he had thieved Mollie's underwear. The wearing of that had made him feel both self-conscious, but also strangely proud and happy. Maybe he should follow that lead.

He went into Mollie's room and opened her drawers. Like Mollie, all a little in disorder, to say the least. A sudden sense of revulsion had him slamming the door shut. He would do this on his own terms and not by stealth. Returning to the desk, he clicked onto an underwear firm. He would have his own things, not steal. Eagerly he created an account and went shopping.

Chris wasn't the only one in a mess on that

morning. Mollie didn't like new starts, especially when it was in something she had neither the training nor experience in. The dogs were keen, though, and were breathing down her neck as she negotiated the back lanes. She would only drive past the stables to The Manor when she felt more secure. She parked and, with bouncing dogs, went to the back door as told. Poking her head in the kitchen, there was nobody around; the house was silent. Not even Joanna's dogs replied. Had she come on the wrong day? She let the dogs into the back garden as instructed and made her way into the main house. In the quiet, she could hear someone being sick. Following the sounds, she found Joanna heaving over the loo.

'Can I help?'

Joanna jumped out of her skin, looked around, then retched again. Mollie got a cup of water.

'Would this do?'

Joanna took the cup and sipped. 'Thanks, hopefully this won't last long.' She sat on the edge of the bath, white as a sheet. 'Not a good start to the working day. I was going to have our morning all worked out.' She leapt up and returned the water to the loo.

'Maybe you need to see a doctor. There was all this talk about Kate Middleton when she had her babies, how she suffered from extreme morning sickness.'

'I'll give it a bit longer!' Her colour seemed to return at this point. 'Guy is out with the dogs;

he couldn't stand the noise. First thing, could you change our bed linen and put it in the wash?' Mollie wasn't too keen on this sort of personal thing, but it couldn't be worse than mucking out. Joanna showed her the laundry room, laid out with wooden shelving and painted in cream paint. 'It's all authentic; we've gone into every detail. Lovely, isn't it?' Mollie had to agree, then laden with sheets, off she went. She gritted her teeth. This was someone's personal life, too intimate, but she got herself into professional mode, thinking it like a holiday let and did the job swiftly.

Joanna was talking to the dogs in the back garden. 'I feel much better in the fresh air! What I want us to do this morning is empty the bedroom next to ours. It will be the nursery. It was my room as a kid and we haven't touched it so far.'

They trudged back up the stairs. The room was small but covered in Take That posters and the small bed had a Take That duvet on it. There were pony books, too and rosettes pinned on the wall.

'I'm going to be brutal! We're going to do this in pale green, with this cupboard darker. It will be a temporary home as she/he will have the room along the landing when she's bigger. This will do for the broken night phase!'

So they bundled it all up. Mollie was just grabbing a big red and blue rosette.

'No, leave that one; it was the last one that Challenger won before I blew it all. Oh, and we've just heard that Dad and Diane will be back next week for a flying visit, so we'll have to make ready the guest room.' They looked around. The room seemed bigger.

'What about all these books? Ooh, you've got an original Silver Snaffles. Do you know this can cost over £100?'

'No! Some of these were my mother's, some mine, and I still read them when I need a comfort read.'

'I've got all mine, too, somewhere at my parents' place. Maybe I should get them back. What are we doing with these, then?'

'A place of honour in the library, I think. I've got some more in a cupboard in the kitchen.'

They gathered all the old clothes from the cupboard and made a heap on the landing. Joanna groaned and slumped on the bed. 'It's no good; I'm beaten.'

'Have you eaten today?' Joanna raised an eyebrow at her, and Mollie giggled. 'Why don't you go to the kitchen and I'll lump all this stuff to its destinations. Did you say the bed and rug are going, too?'

Joanna nodded and took herself off, leaving Mollie, who at last felt she was being appreciated for what she was doing. As she was returning from dumping the mattress, Mollie found herself under the watchful gaze of a tall, red-haired man. He suddenly smiled. 'Hi, I'm Guy. We haven't met yet. Joanna's other half.' They formally shook hands. 'Your dogs are well behaved. I've just put our two out with them; no bouncing or barking at me. Very impressed, but no good as guard dogs!'

Mollie sniggered. 'I was a bit worried, as I've heard about your dog training. So I'm not going to be told off?'

'I'm sure I'll find something!!' But he was grinning.

'I've still got a bed frame to carry downstairs. Could you help me?'

'Of course; the nursery. How is she?'

'Throwing up like mad when I arrived, then she went weak, so I've sent her to the kitchen to eat.'

'You sent her? That's a first, her following instructions without arguing. I can see you're going to be invaluable here!' Together they lugged all the bed stuff downstairs, Mollie partially terrified she would damage something preciously Victorian. Guy was quiet, too, probably being careful for the same reasons. They found Joanna in the kitchen cooking something messy.

'Anyone for soup?' Mollie looked at the clock. It was nearing lunchtime.

'Yes, please, breakfast seems a long time ago.'

'How's Chris doing? Haven't seen him for a while at our home group?'

'He's fine. He's been teaching me to milk. I bought him a laptop for his birthday, and he's been permanently on it in the past few days.'

The other two looked astonished.

'He's the original Luddite technophobe. Well, he might actually move into this century at last!'

smiled Joanna. 'We worry for him a bit; he's been so on his own. And now, of course, the village is full of rumour and scandal that you've moved in!'

Mollie knew she couldn't do anything with these two but tell them the whole story of the compromise living, but she kept off Chris's reasons. He would have to tell people that himself.

'I knew Liz can be a bit difficult. I'll have to tell Diane about this when they arrive.'

'Really, I don't want to cause problems for anyone. I guess I may have been at fault, too.'

'But she is running the place for Diane, and she must keep certain standards. Keith isn't actually her horse, and I'm not sure that Diane will be over the moon that he was running wild all summer.'

'I didn't realise that. I thought the whole place was hers to run. I've only been there a year or so.'

'Don't worry, I'll be discreet! Now that I seem to have a rush of energy, shall we get on with the nursery? Guy has the wonderful flat pack job of the cot and the furniture; we just have to slap the paint on. I know it's months away, but I will then have the fun of the curtains and buying all the baby stuff.' Joanna looked a little dreamy.

'No problem, but could I just take the dogs for a quick run up the lane? They've been in the garden, but Mutantmutt won't do her stuff at home for some reason!' She saw Joanna send Guy a warning look, Mollie guessed to stop him going into dog training mode. They smiled, leaving Mollie feeling not only a little jealous, but also happy inside.

The afternoon was spent getting covered in pale green paint, as Mollie found she got just as messy painting as when she was mucking out. However, the room looked lighter when they had finished. Joanna began muttering about carpets, as they had found her old one worn in places.

'I'm not going to argue with her,' laughed Guy as he ripped it up. At least I hadn't brought the furniture in! Mollie drove home, reflecting on how she had found it the most relaxing and pleasant day she had ever spent at work. No ranting, no rushing around to get rides out, losing bits of tack, then scrambling to get everything done to go home at a reasonable time. And she was being paid for it. Wonderful. The dogs were tired, so no need for a walk. She had enjoyed the easy banter between Guy and Joanna. Had her parents been so when she was on the way? She doubted it.

The familiar cold feeling swept across her as she thought about her family. Had her childhood been normal? She had just taken it as so. The little that Chris had told her had changed her perspectives. She pondered as she drove. The succession of nannies before she went to school; why had she been sent as a weekly boarder at 8? That feeling of never quite belonging that hung over her time there revived its head, but at least it wasn't as bad as the homesickness some had suffered. What had happened to Tricia, she wondered? Like most of the girls, she had also been a daughter of a diplomat or a service family, and, like the others, vanished after a couple of years. Probably married with kids that she was now sending to boarding school despite all she had said. Mollie could feel again the disappointment of each summer when her parents would say it was inconvenient with the business and leave her in school, or get her to find someone to beg to stay with. She hadn't been alone in this. They had all been adrift. The lost girls, they'd called themselves. They had found fags and booze, often freely available in other don't care parents' houses, along with lost boys, and they had steadfastly ignored all that the church, school and nuns had warned them against.

That summer. Mollie felt warm again. Tricia and her horses. Discovering ponies and the fun that entailed. So much so, that with an unheard-of bravery, in the autumn she had insisted to her parents that she had riding lessons. They surprisingly caved into her insistence, and being them, had indulged her. Had it all been just to keep her out from under their feet? Life became essence of horse as she read, lived and breathed them until she left school and insisted that she went and trained as a riding instructor. Her parents had refused to fund her original wish to get into show jumping, and this seemed the next best option. She wasn't academically minded.

Those years, horses 24/7. Mollie could see herself that morning of the final exams when she had thrown up before completing the cross country course. Her first job at a jumping yard, then a dressage yard where she had really been no more than a glorified groom, then Liz. The sheer hard work had tired her passion, but it had only gone underground. That free gallop on Dixie had brought her zing back again. Now she could enjoy horses again. Maybe she could buy one for herself...

TWELVE

Mollie woke suddenly and looked at her clock. No, it wasn't milking time, not her turn. What was going on? She could now hear Chris's boots thundering up the stairs. He burst through the door, starting the dogs barking. 'You've got to come; those daft cows are both calving at once, right in the middle of the muddiest bit of the field and I can't move them, as they're both fighting over one calf while Ziggy has two hooves sticking out!' He turned and went back out. Mollie struggled into clothes, and when she got downstairs and put her boots on, she also heard it was pouring down with rain. She struggled through the field to where she could see Chris's torchlight.

'What do you want me to do?'

'We both need to lift this calf and they'll follow.'

They struggled with the slippery object, but it was not good. There was nothing to catch hold of; its weak limbs just slipped out of their hands and it was made worse by the two mothers bellowing and getting aggressive with the interference. Mollie had a brainwave.

'Why don't you get the tractor with the bucket and put the calf in that? I don't think the truck or the Land Rover will get through this slop.' Chris didn't argue, and Mollie stood over the calf trying to keep some of the rain off it. The roar and two headlights came like a dragon through the darkness. Chris slowly lowered the bucket and then they both slid the poor creature into it. Queenie and Ziggy stood breathing fiercely over it, so Chris backed gently down the field towards the barn. At least the other cows weren't in the field to cause more confusion. Slowly, they slipped and ground their way into the barn. Mollie threw the doors open while Chris turned the tractor around so that the bucket went in first. Both the cows barged past Mollie, nearly knocking her flying, but she grabbed the tractor, muttering under her breath. Chris lowered the bucket to the floor, and the calf slid gently onto the straw. Mollie switched the light on. Both cows were now trying to wash the poor creature, when really what it needed was warming up.

'I've seen this in sheep, but never before with cows, the daft old bats.'

'But which one is the Mum?'

'Well, I should guess that it's Queenie, as Ziggy has the hooves still stuck. We can't wait around. We need to warm it up and quickly.' Chris grabbed some straw and barged his way through to the calf and began pummelling it. Mollie joined in.

'We really need some blankets or something, or a stall with an infra-red heater. Hey, did you have a foaling box when the horses were here?'

'Just across the yard,' said Chris breathlessly. 'But I don't know if there's a lamp and even how we will get the two of them in there. Have a look; it's the last stable on the right.' Mollie went out and switched on the yard light. The stable was very dusty, but there was a lamp. She got a broom and brushed the cobwebs off and switched it on. Apart from the smell of burning dust, it worked. She fetched a couple of bales and set a deep bed. Rushing back into the barn, she found that things had moved on. Ziggy was now lying in the corner, with her own birth taking place. The calf was groggily trying to stand, and Queenie was anxiously nudging it.

'I've put the light on in the box, but maybe we don't need it now?'

'No, the calf really is too cold, her ears are frozen.'

They watched the slow progress towards the udder until at last she latched on and drank.

'Go and get a feed bucket and we'll walk them across the yard to the box.'

Queenie was happier now she had fed her baby and remembered the joys of the feed bucket. Soon, the two were beginning to gently steam in the box. Chris shut the door with a sigh of relief. 'Sometimes I just get really sick of these stupid animals, their innate death wishes and cussed mindedness; then they produce something cute and I weaken! We better go back and see how Ziggy is doing.'

Little progress had been made, obvious even to Mollie's inexperienced eyes. Ziggy was straining and getting nowhere.

'That's just what I need. Before we call the Vet, I'm going to have to shove my hand up. Bleurgh! Mollie, could you get the clean bucket from the cupboard at the back of the dairy? Hot water please and there's a box with all the stuff I need in it.'

When she returned, Chris, with a big shiver took all his outer layers off except his t-shirt and began to wash his hands. Mollie fetched a halter and stood ready at the other end. As Chris thrust his hand in, Ziggy arched her back and flooded Chris in wet smelliness. Undaunted, Mollie could see him gently feel around, all the time murmuring to her gently.

'It's such a big calf, we're going to have to help her. He stood back and put a jumper on. In the box, he pulled out an odd looking contraption with rope and bits of metal which he tied around the feet. He waited. Then when the next contraction came, he pulled.

'It's no good. You're going to have to come and help. Tie her to that ring,' barked Chris. Mollie came around and he showed her how to pull with a downward motion. They took tension and waited. When it came, they pulled in unison. Mollie could feel the stuck-ness of the calf and then the sudden give as it slipped forward.

'Keep the tension up!' shouted Chris as he felt her slacken a bit. Then, with a rush, the calf came through. Its shoulders twisted, and it fell to the ground. Chris went straight to its nose and cleared it. He then rubbed it, but it wasn't really necessary, as the calf took a breath, snorted snot and gunge all over him and began to struggle up. 'Let her go!' Mollie released Ziggy, who turned on a sixpence to greet her new baby. 'Such a large one; don't think there will be any problems there!' Chris sighed with relief as it was already on its feet. 'And another heifer, not bad at all.'

Mollie was spellbound. She'd never had such contact with birth, and she was just bowled over that animals could show so much love. It was almost a comfort to her to see the sweeping wipes of Ziggy's tongue. 'It's amazing. I never saw this dimension to cows or even any animals before.'

'As I said, they drive you nuts, then they do this! Hang on. Something's not right.' Ziggy was turning around, and her tail was in the air. They went to look and saw another pair of hooves protruding and with a rush, another calf slid to the floor. Poor Ziggy didn't know what to do, which one to clean and which one to feed. Chris and Mollie, as one went to clear the airways. This calf was much smaller and lay there not trying to do anything. Chris got rougher, pulling the forelegs backwards and forwards to move the chest. At last, there was a breath and the calf groggily raised her head. Ziggy began to love her, her rough tongue bringing the life into her. She was fine, rising slowly to her feet and wobbling to the teats with a weak determination.

'We've never had twins before with this cross. Three heifers in one night. My gabber has never been so flasted!' laughed Chris. 'And despite her late arrival.' Ziggy was moving the calves into a corner as they both had fed. With a lurch came the afterbirth. Chris got a shovel and took it to the muck heap. 'Foxes are welcome to it!' Leaving the maternity ward, they went to check on Queenie. In the warm box, the now dry mother and baby were dozing, so Chris turned the heater down.

'So now we'll have to think of names,' said Mollie with a smile. 'You aren't going to send these ones away or separate them after all this, are you?' She fixed him with the stare she had used to browbeat her parents. It worked. She had never felt so sure of herself, and passionate, if that was the right word. Chris gulped a bit. 'I suppose so. You are upturning my carefully ordered life, you know. Is nothing sacred?'

'Nope! Had you noticed it's stopped raining and the other cows are waiting to come in?' Chris muttered something under his breath and they both went to the dairy. Mollie felt a little like a zombie as she went through the now- becoming-routine routine and it seemed to go on forever. Chris must have been feeling the same way, too, as she actually saw him slap Patience. Still, at last it was done, and the equipment hung up. They made their way slowly across the yard.

'You know, we do seem to make a good team!'

Mollie suddenly found a welling up of hope and humour. 'We're really colour co-coordinated, slime and mud!' They looked at each other and giggled. Both were wet, tired and unwashed, and suddenly very tired. 'I think a fry up is in order, and then maybe a nap. So what if it's only 8.30? Our time's our own!' laughed Chris. 'But if I cook, you can sort the washing up.'

'Sexist nonsense. I cook, you wash.' Bantering, they went into the house where the dogs greeted them in a frenzy at having missed out on the fun and their breakfast. This was made worse when the front door bell rang. Chris was already heading towards the laundry, so Mollie went to the door surrounded by the leaping dogs, who, as she opened the door, rushed out to bark at the caller.

To Mollie's horror, standing on the doorstep was James with a bouquet of flowers in his hand. In that split second, Mutantmutt also recognised him and remembered him, so she did just what she had last time and rushed at the back of his legs. It had the same effect, too, as James was hurled onto Mollie who once again went flying backwards. But this time she went down fighting. Before they hit the floor, her hand was at his face and a hard slap met skin. She also was twisting and turning to get away from him, and she was screaming for Chris.

James fought back, too, wresting himself away, so by the time Chris arrived, the dogs were still barking, but they were both sitting on the carpet.

'Just what the hell is going on?'

'This is the swine who caused me to lose my job and claims I stole his picture which he must have lost!'

'I have come to apologise,' said James coldly, getting to his feet and rubbing his face. 'Not to be assaulted again.'

'Nothing less than you deserve.' yelled Mollie. 'Now get out of here, before I really set the dogs on you.'

'There's no need for that.' He suddenly began to smile and held out his hand to Chris. 'I'm James and I've just come to collect my property.'

'We don't have any of your things here and you're not welcome.' Chris was squaring himself up, which wasn't much good as he was half the width and height of James. Mollie had told him the whole story, well, most of it.

'Now, look, can we be adult about this?' Mollie could see James was trying to keep civil, but she still wanted to go on with the punch up.

'We have nothing of yours here. Just go.' She noticed the dogs chewing the bouquet to pieces and suddenly wanted to laugh.

'Your parents have told me that you have all the furniture from the cottage.' So, they had checked up on her. 'In the cottage was a small writing desk, yes? Do you still have it?'

Mollie nodded.

'Well, while I am writing, I do get a little absent minded, and absorbed in my work.' He looked at them as if expecting their approval. It didn't come.

'I got fed up with the sight of the picture one day and put the picture in the small drawer under the drop down leaf.'

She could see the desk in her mind's eye but wasn't going to give an inch.

'I would really appreciate if we could just go and look at it. Then I can claim my property and leave you in peace.' It was sort of reasonable. Mollie and Chris exchanged a glance. They were getting good at this.

'It's all down in the far barn. It's muddy after last night. I'll get our boots,' said Mollie, not wanting to be alone with the creep. She now put the dogs in the kitchen. The three of them made their way through the puddles and into the barn. Everything was covered in old tarpaulins and feed bags. So, of course, the desk was right at the back. Chris and Mollie clambered over things and heaved a huge box off the desk.

'What the dickens is in this?' Chris struggled.

'My DVDs, maybe we should have a root through them. Leave the box on the side. There's one of books somewhere, too.' There was a clearing of throat from by the door, so they got back on track. Mollie pulled the desk free and pulled at the little drawer. She had forgotten about this semi-secret drawer when they had searched. There inside was his picture, its frame a little worse for wear. It looked like it had been dropped. She clambered back and handed it over. James lit up.

'I'm so relieved to get this back. It used to belong

to my father.' He was smiling broadly. 'Right, well, I'll be on my way. I'm staying in the village for a couple of days. Maybe I could treat you to dinner as a thank you?'

'No, mate, be on your way. You've done enough damage.'

James didn't argue and strode away to where they could see a very new and very clean car parked in the lane.

'Thanks, Chris, you were a star. And I got a good slap in, too!'

''You didn't! Hope you caught him a good one!'

They grabbed the boxes of books and DVDs and went in for breakfast.

James drove away with a chuckle. The dealer he was bargaining with online could now have the images he wanted. Maybe it would up the price a bit. Then, once the money was safely in his bank account, he was sorted for at least a year or so; well, maybe not somewhere to stay. His folks had told him to get out again and the last girl was now ironing for someone else. More film rights were coming in, so he didn't have to produce another book for six months. Holiday time after all the crap he'd had to go through. All that stupid therapy, finding yourself, keeping clean. Well, maybe he should have been an actor, as he'd duped every single one of them. He rubbed the favourite little tin which was, as usual, in his pocket.

The hotel he was staying in would do for the moment; it was up to his usual standard. But golf and swimming he knew would bore him after a while. He needed a new sort of challenge. Mollie. Now that would be a challenge. Firstly, to get her away from that god bothering wimp. If what they said about him in the pub was true, he probably wasn't interested, anyway. Then to get her back for that slap. He vaguely remembered bedding her and it had been good. But most of all; revenge. If he hadn't had a totally brilliant solicitor, he might have been done on that dangerous driving charge. Then, when he had her sorted, he'd walk away. Brilliant. Life was good.

THIRTEEN

Mollie and Chris were leaning over the stable door, admiring the new calf. She was now wearing her standard plastic earrings with numbers and seemed none the worse for her soaking. Mollie had found the process with the ears cruel, but the calf seemed happy. She was now doing preliminary jumps about the box.

'We'd better put them in the barn before they get used to this luxury accommodation. I suppose we must think of names now. Ziggy and Queenie were some of Dad's last ones, and these were his favourite groups, well, Ziggy was David Bowie. Seeing as you have turned everything on its head, I'm handing the duty over to you.'

Mollie pondered for a minute. She felt a silly upsurge of affection for the jumping baby, but her sense of humour cracked in. 'I would rather like Slimy, or is that too like Ziggy?'

'Don't think so. That's settled then. Let's get them into the barn.'

Using a feed bucket as a lure, the two were quickly trotted across the yard into the barn. Queenie had now changed her tune; she wanted nothing to do with her old mate and lowered her head to butt. Chris intervened with a shout and a shove and she backed off, to stand glowering in the corner. Not the same for her two babies. Also wearing their earrings, they all got together to sniff each other and stick their tongues out to test if they were all good. This time Chris and Mollie leant on the wall.

'Go on then.'

'I'm not doing the gooey pair name thing… the larger has a stripe down her face, so Stripe, hopefully, she won't turn into a gremlin. Then the other is Two. How's that?' She felt strangely proud at her ownership. Before Chris could reply, her phone bleeped, and she had to look. 'Well, blow me down! It's a text from that James. *Just listen to this; I do so wish to really apologise for all the misunderstandings. Could we meet on neutral ground one evening so I can explain everything? XX James.* How did he get my number? My wretched parents I suppose…. Oh, no, maybe not. He had it when he was staying in the cottage. Rats, what do I do, Chris?'

'Don't get into a conversation. Once they've got you hooked, they won't give up. Block his number.'

'Let me guess, the Riding Club again?'

Chris grinned. 'I'm a past master at dodging unwanted people!'

Mollie sorted her phone out and thrust it back in her pocket. 'That's easily sorted. I'll brief Mutantmutt on knocking him over from the front and preferably by the muck heap. I'm off to work now. Do I need to fetch anything from the shop as I come home, or shall we supermarket on Friday?'

'Friday! See you later.'

Mollie drove out of the yard, today without the dogs as Joanna had said there would be visitors and it would just be easier.

Chris watched her go and again was straight off to his PC. In the past few days, he had gone on exploring this dangerous, odd underworld that he had discovered. There was some sort of need in him. Was it looking for love, but he didn't know where or how? One of the things was an LGBT group, and he was wondering if anyone had contacted him or asked to be his friend. To his joy, there was a message from a bloke called Sandy. He looked at his profile, just seemed a regular bloke, a plumber who lived in Southampton. He sent off a preliminary email saying hi, not giving much more away than his profile. Maybe, at last, he could talk to someone who would understand his dilemma.

Now at a loose end in the wait for a reply, he got up and paced around. What had he done with his time before Mollie? Then a flood of guilt washed over him. He had spent far more time reading his Bible and doing various studies, something he hadn't been able to do since he left the college, but they sent him regular mailings. It was as if he couldn't look God in the eye with all he was up to, as if He didn't know. Then inspiration struck, and he found the college online. He spent a happy time looking at the photos of the courses, the house, the grounds. It all seemed so familiar even though he was there such a short time. He looked at the courses and found it was now possible to take some he had signed up for all that time ago, online. There were webinars, and he found himself signing up for a couple. Why not? With Mollie's help he wasn't permanently tired. He could do this. Something leapt inside him. This was good. In contrast, all his poking around with the gender groups seemed a bit sullied. No, he wouldn't give that up; it wasn't something there would be a course about.

The dogs barked. There was a delivery van in the yard, and he heaved an internal sigh of relief that Mollie wasn't there to collect it, even more so when he saw the firm's name all over the packaging. That would have been difficult to explain. He leapt up the stairs and opened the fragrant package. First of all, he tried on the bra and giggled at his reflection in the mirror. He stuffed socks inside and pranced about. Then the panties, which he knew he'd like. Then the blouse and then the skirt. Shame there weren't any shoes, and he hadn't thought about tights- but he'd worn combinations for years in the winter for farm work.

He went into his parents' room where there was a full-length mirror. He stood and looked and turned. He liked the feel of the clothes, but it was his hair and face that was wrong. Abruptly, he turned and went into the bathroom. He took Mollie's hairspray and flicked his hair back out of his face, so it didn't look like a mop. Then he saw a bag of makeup. Surely a brief look wouldn't do any harm? He tried some lipstick on and gasped at the clown that was in the mirror. Maybe that wasn't such a good idea. He rummaged in the bag and found a gentler tone, which looked better. But he didn't feel at ease looking such a feminine woman. Just what did he want? Was he actually full of testosterone after all? It wasn't much better in the bedroom. How he wished he had someone to talk to about the mess in his head.

Mollie walked into a bit of a dilemma at work, too. Poking her head around the kitchen door, she found four people with cups of coffee. Joanna, still looking pale, rose to greet her.

'Hi, Mollie, just in time to catch these two before they fly off again. This is my dad, Ray.' A tall, bespectacled man stood and shook her hand. 'Glad someone will be around to help Joanna. She takes on too much; she should be resting at the moment. Now, this is my wife, Diane'. The slim woman, with brown hair smiled but didn't get up. They were both spectacularly bronzed. 'We just breezed in for a couple of days, and now we're off to Canada to see the Rockies,' she suddenly explained, as if reading Mollie's mind.

'Can't seem to tie these two down for five

minutes,' smiled Guy. 'Black coffee?' He asked to break what seemed to be becoming an awkward silence, especially as Joanna had suddenly bolted.

'You've got to get her to the doctor. At this stage of the pregnancy, she should be over all this…but then again it may do no good. Her mother was just the same. But things have changed. Mollie, can you try?' asked Ray.

'Me? I'm just Friday. I thought this Chloe was coming?'

'My mum?' asked Diane. 'She's at a conference until next week.'

'I'll try, but I don't know anything about babies!!'

'Look, we don't have long, Ray. I need to talk to Mollie about the stables,' said Diane firmly.

Mollie panicked.

'I've heard that there was an accident at the yard in the summer, and you ran the place until Liz returned, and then she sacked you? That Keith was running up at Chris's place all summer under your supervision?'

'No, that's not quite right.' Mollie was stung. 'I was detailed to take the mares up to Chris's place before it all happened. I was the only one with a trailer license. After I was sacked, yes, I went to share the house with Chris, as I was needing somewhere to live. But I haven't spoken to Liz since, and Keith was never my responsibility. After the accident, I worked seven days a week through the whole summer without a break. Liz insisted I was there, and I had a meltdown with exhaustion.

She walked in on it and sacked me, as she thought I was carrying on with her husband.'

'And were you?' Demanded Diane.

'I resent that! I most certainly wasn't. Who are you to cross-examine me?' Mollie rose from her chair, 'I'm sorry, Guy, but this is no one else's business but mine.'

'Take a breath, Mollie,' he put his hand on hers. 'Diane can be abrupt, can't you?' He glared at her.

'My apologies,' she said stiffly. 'But you must understand my position. Liz has a contract with me to run the yard and the breeding scheme. Keith is the last in an important line of Welsh cobs, and his bloodline will soon die out if we don't use him. I have been very selective in the mares and need him to be fit and well. Running wild on a hillside is not what I expected.'

'But Chris is experienced with a stud. He looked after him really well.'

'That's not the point. He was supposed to be stabled and exercised from the yard.'

'Well, I had nothing to do with the decision; all I did was follow orders.'

'I also spoke to some girl, Tina? She seemed to think she was the yard assistant, but I hadn't cleared her for that job.'

'Was I checked?'

'I saw your CV and followed up your references, yes.'

'Then why did I never get a contract?'

'One was sent to you. Was that why you walked

out?'

'There was nothing to keep me there. Tina thought she could run everything and had undermined me the whole time, so why should I stay?'

'I see…' Diane looked a little uncomfortable. 'Perhaps it was never such a good idea to extend the yard if I'm not going to be able to keep a close eye on things. We had planned to go back into the Equine-assisted therapy but couldn't find anyone qualified. Now I'll have to re-think it all again.'

'Well, maybe if you stayed put in one place for more than six months at a time, you wouldn't get things in such a pickle.' Joanna returned to the room. 'And I'm not going to the doctor's to be given medicines that might have horrible after effects or be made to lie in bed. It is getting better.' She glared at everyone. 'So what are you going to do about the yard?'

'There's not much I can do until her contract comes up for renewal. Keith is back on the yard and I've read her the riot act about looking after him properly. Could you go down now and then and take a look, Mollie?'

'You must be kidding. I haven't set foot on the place since I left. I'm not even going to drive in here this way. I come over the hill.' Mollie felt maybe she had revealed too much.

'I'm doing it again, aren't I, Ray?'

'What, being bossy and controlling? Yup!' He was smiling. 'Say sorry to everyone and we must go for that flight!'

'Sorry!' This time she smiled genuinely. 'And sorry especially, Mollie, I can't help it!'

'We know,' chorused the others, and the ice was broken with laughter. Nevertheless, Mollie was relieved when Ray and Diane left and the house was in peace again. She did some washing up and waited for Joanna to return.

'I do apologise for my mother in law!'

'It's all right; it was just a bit of a shock being cross-examined. What do we have to do today?'

'Can you sort out their bedroom and do the washing? I have some emails to deal with.' Smiled Joanna.

This was safer ground, so Mollie scuttled and got working. There wasn't much to do, so she found herself driving home early, keeping to her hilltop route. She felt a bit annoyed and partially vindicated, but it was easy to let it go. She would take a walk with the dogs and blow it all away.

'Chris, hey, where are you, do you fancy a walk?'

The house was quiet, but his truck was there. He had to be somewhere around. She heard something upstairs; he could be in his attic. She bounced up the stairs and burst into his bedroom.

'Don't come in, I'm not decent!' He shoved the door hard against her, so she couldn't get in. But she had seen enough. Chris was wearing women's underwear. She waited outside, but he was quiet.

'Are you Ok?'

'You saw, didn't you?' he said through the door.

'Yes, look, I couldn't care less, but if you need to talk…'

'You're not shocked? Disgusted?'

'I went to a Catholic boarding school. I've seen some things that would make your hair stand on end! Come on down to the kitchen and I'll put the kettle on.' She thundered downstairs, so he would know she was gone. Poor bloke. So that was why he was such a loner. That was why the Riding Club was after him; they all wanted a gay best friend. Or was he? All this gender equality stuff was in the media, but she hadn't really paid much attention to it. But he was Chris, probably the best friend she'd ever had, ever. It also explained why she wasn't attracted to him.

Chris was shaking in his bedroom. All so suddenly in the open. What was she going to say, even though she had been kind? He sighed. Maybe it was better that it was all out in the open. He couldn't face going downstairs yet, but he had to. He felt a bit like a naughty child caught eating or stealing. But, no, he wasn't going to back down if she thought he was nuts. The bra had to go, one sock was falling out and it really didn't feel right to him. The thong was though. He dressed, took a deep breath, and to his surprise found himself saying 'Help me, Lord', as he went down the stairs.

FOURTEEN

Chris was shaking like a leaf by the time he reached the kitchen and was glad of the warmth. He didn't know what to say, so he just sat down in the armchair.

'Don't look so terrified! What do you think is going to happen?'

'I don't know…it's the being found out, that I'm not normal.'

'Well, no one's that these days. Have you been on the Internet about all this? Was it my computer coming that changed this? If so, I'm sorry.'

'No, I think it's good. Yes, I've been going around all the websites, looking and trying to find where I relate to all this.'

'All this? Get it all off your chest.' Mollie handed him a coffee laced with whiskey. He was as white as a sheet, despite the tail ends of the makeup. He took a big sip and shuddered.

'I…I…saw your underwear one day and just suddenly wanted to see what it felt like to wear.'

'And?' He looked even more embarrassed.

'I don't go much on the bras, but I find a thong quite comfy!'

'But you're a bloke!'

'Can we just leave that there?' he squirmed.

Mollie grinned.

'Of course. Putting it on stirred something up; is it having me in the house, too?'

'You're being here has been the best thing that's happened for ages. It's made me realise how I've been living a half-life, an odd life, and now I'm looking for a new normal.'

'Have you contacted anyone in a like place?'

'Not really, but I had an email from a plumber in Southampton. Maybe that will lead somewhere.'

'What is it you need to find out? Is it which way you swing?'

'I suppose so. All my life I seem to have swung in no direction at all. I must go in some sort of way, I suppose.'

'Do you want to be a bloke who wears women's clothes but stays a man?'

'I'm not sure. When I put on the skirt and blouse, it felt fine, but not for me. The makeup made me look like a clown. I guess I'm searching for me.'

'Does me have to be a man or a woman, or something in-between? What did all the websites tell you?'

He took another big gulp. 'That everyone has to be a something, have their own label and identity, a group they can hang out with. None of them felt like me. It's as if I'm in the middle, not knowing what way to go.'

'I can identify with that. I've never fitted in really well at school. It wasn't until I found horses that I found some real friends, but we all seem to have drifted apart. Don't you have mates in the farming community?'

'I think I've told you; they've all married or moved on or are just trying so hard to make a living that they don't have the time for anything.'

'There's always the Riding Club!'

Chris threw a cushion at her.

'Well now, look, you're all in the open now. If you want to wear women's stuff, go for it, but I wouldn't recommend it for milking. I have absolutely no sense of clothes, so I can't be your fashion guru.' She suddenly smiled. 'You know, the first time I came up to the farm, I saw we both have no colour sense. They were always taking the mickey out of me at the stables; I never seem to be able to get the colours right. I would turn up in my favourite purple jodhs with an orange patterned t-shirt not having given it a second thought. You do just the same.' They smiled like conspirators. 'But we can do a trip together to Southampton and do the shops. I don't think anyone cares who buys what in some of these shops. If that's what you want to do?'

'Well, it seems to be a starting point. I don't seem to get any progress in any other way.' He was looking a better colour now.

'I can't really do any more. I know which way I bat, but I really feel for you, and as my best friend – note, I didn't say gay; what you do doesn't matter.'

He now smiled.

'Do you think something happened in your childhood? Your aunt said something strange happened after you were born.'

'What happened?' She told him.

'Most odd, they said nothing about it to me. Now let me think a bit. I can remember always being with Mum and Dad, following them about the farm. We're a bit isolated up here, but kids would be about to play with the horses. Mum was always in dungarees like Dad, so I've no idea why I liked the skirts…They did once buy me a Sindy doll. That seems odd, but they said I should try all things out. School. I was there only a year before Mum insisted on teaching me at home.'

'Did you know why they decided on that?' She let him think.

'No idea. Mum said she thought I would learn better at home because the standard was so low. The Rev Jones told me that, too. Hey, the Reverend Jones, I'd forgotten all about him. He was a trendy vicar, and we had lots of guitars and happy-clappy music in church. He would come for lunch now and then, and he would take me for a walk, or we would see the ponies afterwards.'

Mollie raised her eyebrows, and he took her point.

'You're thinking of some sort of childhood abuse? It's all the rage at the moment, isn't it! But no, my memories are of a good, gentle man. Hey, we can check him out!'

A simple search on an Anglican website found

he had moved from church to church, never staying long in one place, but he was loved by each community for his love and innovation. He had been pivotal in some court cases where the social services had tried to take children away from families, and it seemed that in most cases he was successful.

'But nothing like that happened to you, did it?' asked Mollie peering over his shoulder.

'If it happened, I was totally unaware. I have no memories of jobsworth people visiting and having meetings. I wonder if we will find anything if I type in their names?' He realised they were off the track a bit, but this was just as interesting and took the pressure off. The cases didn't seem to have been newsworthy, as the children had remained with families. The Reverend was single; the trail seemed to have ended.

'Where do we go from here? What would you like, Chris?'

'I would just like to be able to go on exploring as I was, but now without guilt, and with your patience and your makeup bag.'

That's OK with me. But I have one question.' Mollie took a deep breath. 'Are you a man, a woman, or gay?'

'That's a blinder. I don't know.'

He was saved by the arrival of another delivery van, but this time the parcel was for Mollie, who was puzzled, as she hadn't ordered anything.

They took the parcel into the kitchen and

unwrapped it. Inside was a simple silk dress in a pale blue motif. They both breathed 'wow' at the same time.

'I didn't order this! Is this something for you, but the wrong name, you sneaky thing?'

'Not guilty; can you see me wearing this? I haven't even got as far as frocks.' Mollie held it up. It glistened in the light. Chris was scrabbling in the wrapping. 'Listen to this.'

'Dear Mollie, everything went so wrong the other day when I came around to visit you and collect my painting. I'm so sorry for the mistakes and misunderstandings. I would really be honoured if you would join me for dinner one night at the Crown Hotel. No ties, no begging, no falling over, just a chance to explain all that has happened to me since that time I was with you. It's an apology and a thank you. Just a one-off meeting to clear the air. I would be so honoured.

James

'That's a real one for the books, isn't it? The slimy so-and-so, well-crafted to put the boot on the other foot as it were,' said Chris. Mollie sighed.

'It's a shame I can't stand him. Even the thought of him has my toes curling! Do you think there's any chance this is genuine?' she said wistfully.

'My every instinct says no. There was just something about him I couldn't take to. But if you need to find out, go. If anything, it's a free meal. You can always pour whatever fancy drink he gives you over his head!'

'I could insist that you come, too, though I wouldn't say you were the safety net.'

'Na, I really would like to wipe his face in the muck! You've got this lovely dress to wear.' Now Chris was wistful.

'How about we both try it on? Whoever looks best in it keeps it?'

For a split second, Chris looked confused. 'That really is an option, isn't it? Like a new door opening. You go first.'

They rushed up the stairs to his parents' room, and Mollie went first. It fitted beautifully and went with her brown hair, even though it was in full frizz. She twirled herself in the mirror, then peeled it off and thrust it at Chris. They stood looking at him in the mirror. It suited his blondness as much as Mollie's red. He twirled. He looked. He stopped and ripped the dress off.

'It's not me; I don't want to be a woman. I want to be me, whatever that is, and it's not about wearing a frock.' He stalked out, and Mollie could see that he was near to tears. She went to follow, but some instinct made her let him go. A few minutes later, she heard hooves leaving the yard; the best way for him to work things out. She picked the box up and put the dress back in. Should she go? A small part of her said, why not? It would be a good chance to use someone for a change instead of being used. A night out, with Chris ready to be back up. There was always the possibility James was telling the truth. But she would not be bought, and one thing was certain; it wouldn't be in this dress. She folded it back up, found the paperwork and prepared it to be returned.

Chris came back to the farm a couple of hours later. The mad gallop with Dixie along the lanes, the stretching muscles, mud flying, the watering eyes from the cold wind had soothed his soul. They had both run out of breath at the same time, slowing to a walk and then ambling along. Whatever demons had him leaving the house had flown. He was now suddenly at peace. He had made one decision. He might have a hankering after brightly coloured clothes, some odd underwear, and that was going to be what he was. He was free to choose. If that included some makeup, well, so be it. He suddenly saw his dad's David Bowie albums. He wasn't doing anything new.

It was getting dark, and the lights were on in the milking parlour. He fed Dixie, turned her out and peeked in at Mollie. She was singing to Patience as she stripped her off, two cats waiting for the saucer of milk that would follow. All was in order. She saw him and grinned. In the house he made a coffee and went once again to the computer, already beginning to curse its addictive nature. To his joy, there was an email from Sandy.

Hi! Thanks for replying. I have no experience of being on a farm, having lived all my life in the city. But I guess it's less stressful than mending bogs and pipes. I've been on this site a couple of months and have made some great friends; have you yet? I guess I'm dodging why we're all on it. I don't really like writing about myself; it's so easy to be misunderstood. Would you like to meet up sometime for a pint and a chat? No complications. There's a great club with live music that I go to near the station. What do you think? Drop us a line soon.

It seemed so easy and simple, and perhaps, at last, he could really talk to someone. Mollie, for all her care and love, was still a woman, and how could she know how it felt in his body and mind when she was so? He would reply, but he would sleep on it, as he wanted to be sure he said the right thing. Smiling to himself and suddenly feeling completely drained, he went to cook up something for supper.

Mollie hung up the last of the milking equipment and went to check on the calves, who were asleep in a corner. It was all she could do not to go and lie and cuddle them, but she didn't want to disturb their peace. The mums seemed to have got over their differences and were stuffing their faces with hay. No crying for their lost babies if Chris had won the battle. All was well in their world. Then she noticed Queenie was actually leaking milk from her enormous udder. She must talk to Chris about milking her then.

Ha, an excellent compromise between old and new. That word was grating on her; it seemed to be creeping into all aspects of her life. At least Chris had seemed okay. Poor bloke, what a mess to be in. Yet he had had what she would have called an idyllic childhood. Home with both parents, living on this farm. Horses and dogs all around. Their constancy, even into the home-schooling. She had a sudden picture of her mother with her talon-like nails trying to write on a blackboard or explain something to her without losing her temper. Different worlds, both with their own drawbacks. Jealous of what Chris had, although he had lost it. Would it be better to have had such a great childhood but lose parents, or have hers who had never really been a father and a mother? She was suddenly aware that what she had called normal wasn't. There could have been another way, and she hadn't had it. It was as if Chris's restlessness and his need for clarity about his life were catching.

She suddenly needed to know why her parents were like they were. Why had she spent so much of her childhood in boarding school? Why had they never taken her on holiday with them? Why had it seemed they were avoiding her? Why were they so unaffectionate? Why did it seem they couldn't wait to get rid of her, and now, almost pay her off?

The decision filled her with both panic at what she might find out and facing the actual confrontation. She was scared of them, came the sudden revelation. Wow, why? This firmed up her decision. As soon as she had a free day, she was off to Winchester, unannounced, so they couldn't squeak out of it. She was going to find her peace, even if she was terrified of the process. It would be nice to have such a simple life as the cows had, but would she not get bored without a bit of something to make it more interesting?

FIFTEEN

The day off came sooner than expected, because the next morning Joanna cancelled as she had a hospital appointment and Guy was going, too. First, of all, they had to deal with an un-willing Queenie, who wasn't going to leave her baby and be milked. Even food didn't work. She cavorted around the barn, setting the others off into a round of nuttiness, the calves joining in. Chris was down and grumpy and suddenly went off and returned with a bucket, stool and halter.

'Your idea, you can now hand-milk off the excess. We don't need her to get mastitis. Put this on.' He then haltered Queenie, who was quite happy being tied up in the barn with her baby.

'Now get comfy. Like we do when we strip the last of the milk. She may fight you at first, but she really needs to get rid of this, or else she'll leak. You now have to get a stronger rhythm and don't stop. Watch she doesn't get her foot in the bucket either or we'll have to chuck the milk. There's another clean one over there. Just keep going until she slows, no stripping.'

He stomped off.

Mollie now entered into a new world. Yes, her wrists began to ache, but with her head against the warm cow's side, the rhythm was both relaxing and absorbing. It was a blissful, embryonic feeling. Then her mind turned to her decision. She was going to stick with it, however terrified she felt. When she had said to Chris that she had to visit the parents and pulled a face, he had accepted it at face value. He was now dog minding, too, as her mother didn't like dogs at the best of times. She finished one side and did the other, and released Queenie. Of course, the calf wanted a drink and looked disgustedly at Mollie when she found little on tap. The whole process had soothed Mollie, despite the aching arms, and she was ready for her journey.

The drive to Winchester was for once not clogged with traffic, which was a relief, but she had also hoped that sitting in the car would give her a quiet place to prepare mentally. Of course, there was also the hope that her parents wouldn't be there, and she could shelve the whole mission. Once on the road to Alresford, it all got worse, and she had to pull over for a few minutes; she really was a bundle of nerves. She could do this. She had to find out for once and for all why they were so unloving. Was it something she had done or was it them? That was the nutshell. Fixing on that, she drove down the lane and found herself saying an 'Our Father'. That took her right back to when she had come home from school, so she must have had this dread for many years.

The cottage was unchanged, still looking

chocolate box cute with the thatched roof and tiny windows. Formerly two labourers' cottages, it had been knocked into one. Again, it struck Mollie that she had always had her room on one side of the house and her parents on the other, completely separate. She had only had company when they had guests. So why had they never allowed her to have a friend to stay? It was just turning 11, so it should be a good time to catch them before they went for lunch or the pub. Their Mercedes was parked at the side, too. It was now or never; now was her time. She began to shake, but walked with determination around the side to the back door. This had been her home and she would treat it as such. She opened the kitchen door and called. 'Anyone home?' A voice hailed her from the sitting room, so she went through.

Her mother was sitting with a glass on the coffee table, cigarette in hand, and a blank look on her face. This changed in a flash as she recognised her daughter. The look was of hatred. Mollie took a step back. Her mother's glare was controlled into the familiar disdaining face; with that, she relaxed a bit.

'What are you doing here?' she snarled.

'I was in the area and thought I would pop in and see you.'

'Well, there was no need. I suppose you're after something?'

'Like what?'

'Well, it's usually money or something for those

stinking horses,' her mother sneered. Mollie could now see that she was completely drunk and holding herself together, using anger. She went for it and sat down on the sofa to begin her mission. She had never seen her mother drunk like this, and she would use this to her advantage.

'Actually, I came here because I wanted to ask you something, not for something, but about something.' Her mother remained silent. 'Why do you hate me so much?'

At this, she physically recoiled and grabbed a swig of her drink.

'You always had me looked after by nannies, sent me off to school as soon as you could, never had me on holiday with you, and then paid to get me out of the way as soon as possible by finding the job at the stables. You never let me have anyone to stay but pushed me into going elsewhere. The only time we were together would be Christmas and then you would pack me off again on Boxing Day. So now I demand an explanation.'

'Why now?'

'Don't try to side-track me, tell me.'

At this, her mother actually looked her full in the eyes, which she had never done before. Mollie met the stare full on.

'I wanted a boy.'

The silence went on as the two of them tried to out stare each other. Her mother broke first.

'Never wanted a girl. Wanted a son to carry on the business, to be a hero, a politician, a doctor, a world leader. Not a woman who would go half cracked at a career, fall in love and end up wasting her life being a mother.'

'Just like you did,' sniped Mollie.

'Oh, no, I didn't. Who do you think has run the business all the years? Not just your father, although he would like everyone to think that. No, we made the company the biggest in the country, a world leader. I didn't need you snivelling around the place. I knew as soon as you were born, you would come to nothing; another pathetic woman. You're like your father, who only gets on with things if I keep on pushing him.'

'The only mistake I made was being born? Did you not love me at all?'

Her mother momentarily paused, then sneered again. 'Love has no meaning in my life.'

'If you were running such a wonderful business, why did you need to sell the Hazeley cottages? All that talk about needing some cash for retirement?'

The glare returned. 'Complete rubbish. You weren't making a go of it, so they had to go.'

'But you wouldn't let me run it to make a success of it.'

'We gave you every opportunity. You never fought back. If you had done, things might have been different.'

'You blocked my every move. You would never listen. I saw no point in fighting a brick wall. Was it because you wanted me to fail?'

Her mother rose and re-filled her glass.

'You could never succeed, even if I threw all of our money at you. You wouldn't even consider taking A levels. All you wanted was those wretched horses. No, you were never going to be anything.'

'Did you consider that I could run the company, too? I am your daughter. Or do your own genes mean nothing?'

She didn't answer.

'Didn't Dad have anything to say in all this?'

Her mother snorted the answer.

'Are you going to live forever and no one will have to take over the business when you want to retire?'

'Such a word does not exist in my vocabulary. Your father, yes. He's off playing golf with John.' A sudden, unexpected smile suddenly played on her face and it changed. Mollie got it.

'You've found a me substitute?'

'Could say that. He is the new, fresh blood that will make us real world players. Even now we're playing into the Chinese and Russian markets.'

'So then, why are you so unhappy that at this time of the day you are already on the way to being drunk?'

Her mother took a stride across the room as if she was going to hit Mollie, but with incredible timing, Mollie's dad and the aforesaid John walked into the room. Her mother took that step back and plastered a smile on her face.

'Good game? Both of you look happy! Look who's

popped by. Dear Mollie.'

Mollie's father had the grace to go a little white, but even so, he smiled, too.

'Oh no you don't!' Mollie wasn't going to let this charade play out. She swung to look at John. He was a tall, paunchy, bespectacled man with thinning hair. Quite the vision of a funky leader of industry. She stretched out her hand. 'Hello, John, may I introduce myself? I am Sarah and Peter's daughter.' His hand faltered for a second.

'Pleased to meet you. I understood you were in a wheelchair in assisted living after a riding accident.'

Mollie gasped.

'I think there must have been a misunderstanding,' faltered her father. 'She did have a bad accident a few years ago.'

'No, I didn't. Why is it such a problem for you to have a daughter? Why am I such an embarrassment? I have done nothing to hurt you except to be born!'

'Because I am not letting a woman get her hands on what I have built up!' shouted her mother.

'Do you really think I want it? Did it never occur to you to ask me? I don't want your artificial, kissy, kissy, backstabbing culture. I saw through your fake lives, even when I was a kid. John, you're welcome to them.'

'I think I need to go, as this seems to be a family crisis. It's not my problem.' John turned as if to leave, but Mollie's mother was now between him and the door.

'No, do stay for lunch and we can work these things out between us.'

'What things, Mother?'

'Well, if you really don't want to inherit, we must sort this out.' Boy! Was she quick despite the gin and tonic.

'There's nothing to sort out. Give me a cash settlement now and I'll walk away, and we never need to see each other again.' Mollie's anger was leading her on. 'I'm sure John, this paragon of industry, can do this, and he's bound to have a laptop in his car. We do it now, or I go to the papers.' Mollie was sure of her ground, knowing their dislike of the media. She sat on the sofa and watched the argument that exploded around her. Her father was against it, her mother for it and John was trying to appease them. Eventually, they calmed down.

'We'll give you a quarter of a million. But you have to sign a disclaimer saying you will have no further claim, no further contact. Why a family could be like this, I can't understand. You seem to be the money grabbing person your parents said you were, even before the accident.' said John. Despite his angry tone, Mollie saw a hint of a twinkle. He had her parents sussed. Hopefully, he would take them to the cleaners at some stage and serve them right. This wasn't at all what Mollie had expected. It was like a scene from a cheap melodrama. She couldn't even take on the amount of money. Just how much were they really worth? Didn't really care, because there was a new feeling arising within her and she wanted to hold on to it. John was still talking. 'I have a business cheque here for half the amount, and the balance will be paid when you come to the office on Monday to sign the papers. Will that do?'

'Look, I didn't ask for this much, but I'll take it on principle for my horrible childhood. You know Mother, I'm glad to be gone. It may turn out that I can form a happy, honest relationship with someone, have a loving family and children; give them the best of things that can't be ordered from Harrods. Then I will be richer than you will ever be.' She shook John's hand, and he gave her a card with the address of the solicitors. Her parents, she didn't bother to look at. They would probably celebrate with champagne when she drove away, and she would, too.

Mollie only got as far as the top of the lane before she stopped. She sat there and went through all that had gone by in such a short time. Unbelievable. It was like a scene from a sitcom, but the cheque looked real enough. How did she feel? Was she distressed and wanting to sob? Parents who had never loved her? No, it was a relief. Not to be thinking, Oh no, what do they want this time? She was free in more senses than one. No duty Christmas present exchanging. No more beholden to them. She could be her own person. The problem was theirs. It wasn't anything she had done; it was all down to them. She couldn't be entirely sure until all was signed. Maybe they would try to slip out of it, but she did have the huge carrot of her silence. Mollie started the car and began the drive home. She would buy some champagne, but there was somewhere she wanted to visit first.

Her old school lay on the outskirts of Southampton, and she just wanted to go and have a look. To see how her memories squared up with how it looked. Most of the nuns must have retired by now. They had been so old then, but they had a timelessness about them, it was difficult to tell.

It did indeed seem to have shrunk as she drove up the gravelled drive. The dull, grey building was just as dull and grey. There seemed little sign of life as she parked, but she didn't think it was holidays. She had already forgotten that rhythm. The main entrance had been turned into a reception area, and she found a little grey nun who seemed part of the building manning the desk.

'Hi, I'm an old girl. Is it possible for me to take a walk around the grounds, or is it still term time?'

'Hello, my dear, the place is quite empty. Most of them went home last week. Do have a wander, but watch out for Sister Jo, she can be a bit sharp! I don't recognise you. Perhaps you were here before my time, but we do get old girls popping in now and then. Off you go, but only the big hall is open if you go inside.'

Mollie smiled and made her way to the gardens

at the back. It was here she had smoked her first cigarette, kept her Tamagotchi until it died, and talked horses on end with Tricia. What she wanted to see; was her time at school also so bad? How she was going to discern this, she had no idea. It was an impulse. She sat by the statue of St Anne in the sunshine and just let her memories sweep over her.

'Not another one of the old girls come back again?' said a stern voice. Mollie looked, it was indeed Sister Jo, and she wasn't another day older.

'Hello, Sister, you no doubt don't' remember me, but I do you!'

'But I do. You were the one who had a Tamagotchi behind the Holy Mother. You all thought you were so clever!'

Mollie grinned. 'You were always the scariest one!' It was amazing to be talking to a nun like she was a human being.

'Did you have any contact with my parents?'

'No, they just paid the bills and didn't come to sports day or Mass.'

That kicked off some memories, but she was free of their pull. Two girls walked across the grass giggling until they saw Sister Jo. They quietened down and scuttled off.

'More of the lost girls; not a lot of changes here.'

'You called us that, too? I thought it was our idea.'

'There have always been ones like you. What have you done with your life? Are you married and blessed with children?'

'Not yet. I'm just starting work on a big project. Do you ever hear from Tricia Hughes?'

'No, sorry, her name doesn't come to me, but I remember you because of the Tamagotchi!' They said it together and laughed. For a few minutes more, they talked about the school and nuns, then made their farewells. Indeed, Mollie did have a big project to work on. It would be complete irony after today's events, but it was a great idea. She couldn't wait to tell Chris all about it.

SIXTEEN

Chris was out ploughing when she got back, so Mollie finally made up her mind and replied to James's message in as non-committal manner as you can do by text. She said she would meet him at the Crown Hotel and set the time and date. She was going to set the perimeters on this one. He replied quickly in the affirmative for the following day.

Mollie milked again, but left Queenie, who didn't look anything like as full. She heard Chris drive the tractor into the yard, but he didn't come into the parlour. and went straight into the sitting room and slammed the door. She had so been looking forward to telling him about all that had happened. It was like a slap in the face. But they were just housemates and she had to respect his privacy and feelings. She spent the evening jotting down ideas, searching the internet for similar schemes and costs.

Sitting at his computer, Chris was again cursing Mollie for having brought it into his life. Why did things have to change? He had been slowly adjusting to his parents' deaths and had even begun to feel he could move on. He was now looking at porn sites and felt as if he were drowning in slime, but the feelings it gave him blocked out the misery that was gripping him. Even praying wasn't making any difference and his courses at the Bible school were ignored. The one thing that he had found through all this mess was the realisation that he really wasn't normal physically. It explained all his feelings of confusion, but nowhere could he find an answer as to why and what it was. If his parents had been alive, he probably wouldn't have had the courage to ask them anyway. He was in the same sense too scared to even begin the discussion with Sandy. He was trapped in a sick world that had come upon him so suddenly that he didn't know which way to turn. There was only one way out. He was going to do so much hard work on the farm that when he got inside, he was just going to fall asleep. At least he could do that.

The following morning, Mollie was off to The Manor for an early start. She was going to meet Jan and Harry and they would decide what help would be needed from her when the baby came. Joanna actually looked well when she greeted Mollie. 'It's gone, just like that, overnight, and I feel wonderful!' Mollie thought for a moment, then understood it was the morning sickness. 'You look much better!'

'Come on in. We've already started in the archive.'

Mollie followed her to the back of the house where the new computer room was set up in the old kitchen, which had been Joanna's sitting room. The two men were poring over a box of documents, one tall and dark, the other short with floppy brown hair. Introductions and shaking of hands had Mollie thinking just what nice blokes they seemed.

'Now, we have come to a decision in your absence, I'm afraid!' said Harry with dancing eyes. 'We're going to come down once a week and sort all the boxes as Joanna does, but we're going to want you to just check the emails for queries, so we'll now run you through the programme to show you how to answer. Quite easy, really!' He grinned sideways at Joanna, who rose to the bait.

'It wasn't me who messed up the building records!' They all trooped to the cellar where she was shown the cataloguing system, then back to the computer and they went through the queries.

'It might be that I can manage if you can do the house stuff, but there might be days when I'm tired or have things to do. I just really need to know I have back up,' smiled Joanna. 'Did you really sort it all out, Harry?'

'Yes, we just seem to be missing the bills and records for the building of Chris' farm. It's contemporary with The Manor; the three other farms on the estate were built with the original estate. We can only think that they are somewhere at Chris's place. Could you ask him to have a search?'

'Why are you so interested?'

'Joanna repeated to us all that stuff about it

being the only independent farm on the estate and it being a reward for helping in the great fire.'

'And?'

'We also found out that his family was involved in smuggling and cattle rustling, not to mention there was a highwayman, Black Christopher.'

'Shouldn't you be telling Chris this, not me?'

'I called him the other day and he really wasn't interested. We thought we would try you!' Harry grinned. 'What's the matter with him?'

'Oh, I don't know really; he just seems a bit down at the moment.' Mollie wasn't going to give anything away.

'Will you ask him? We think there have been some dubious doings here in the past.'

'I can but try!' Mollie laughed, and the rest of the morning was spent with cleaning and helping with more baby things.

Driving home, Mollie mused over the whole thing. Was there any way to help Chris? This was all beyond her comprehension. But more on her mind was her upcoming date in the evening. What to wear, as so many signals could be given out, and she always gave the wrong ones. Maybe Chris would help. If not, she decided on some jeans and her only frilly top with a cardigan. She could see it in her mind's eye and the blues and oranges looked fine to her. She would only drink soft drinks; she would have the excuse she was driving and say she mustn't be late due to work, whether true or not. When she drove into the yard, Chris was seeding the field, so she walked up with the dogs to get his attention.

He stopped the tractor and looked down at her. She saw he had bags under his eyes and was looking pale again.

'What?' he barked, and she recoiled. 'Sorry, you just caught me at a bad time.'

'Chris, we have to talk, come in and eat now, and don't argue.' This was her best 'get the stupid kid to do rising trot' voice, and it worked. He turned off the engine and they walked in together. He slumped at the table as she busied herself with the food.

'I know things are getting you down and you have to work through things, but starving yourself and working all hours won't help.'

If only she knew. He took the course he had taken when his mother had been on a tack; he sat there and let her run.

'I'm always here for you. Although I have no idea of what it must be like for you, I can be your sounding board. Saying things out loud instead of letting them go around your head will help. But anyway, pick up your ears and listen to this...'

What Mollie had to say shocked him out of his self-pity. At least his parents had loved him. The money seemed too good to be true. She was as cynical as he would be as to whether there would be more clauses when she went to the solicitors. Then she suddenly changed direction.

'Did you know you had a highwayman as one

of your ancestors and they were involved in smuggling?'

'No idea at all; we didn't really talk about the family beyond the tale of the helping with the fire.'

'Well, it seems that some documents are missing about the building of the farmhouse. Are there any big chests full of secret papers in the attic or hoards of smuggled gold hidden up there?'

'I haven't been up there for ages.'

'Or are there documents in your dad's desk?' She was off on one now. 'After you have eaten this, we're going to have a look! I need this to take my mind off things as well. I'm going to meet James tonight!'

'You WHAT? After all I said?'

The two of them then bickered as they had before, Mollie making sure that she kept Chris's plate loaded as he ate and pointed at her with his fork, reading her the riot act once again, about what a git the bloke was and how he was certain he couldn't be trusted. Inwardly, she heaved a sigh of relief. His pit wasn't so deep that he couldn't be pulled out of it. She made him bring his mug of coffee up to the attic so he wouldn't have a minute to change his mind. They clattered up through his bedroom floor, then up some creaky, windy steps into the roof. At least there was electricity. In the dim light, they stood and surveyed what looked like some ancient boxes with huge padlocks and hasps.

'Looks like the smuggling was real then; these

look like ships' boxes.'

'You and your imagination. They're just old.'

'Well open them, then.' Chris had brought an enormous bunch of old keys that hung in the kitchen. Like a couple of kids, they pushed and shoved, then turned the first key that fitted. All it revealed was a lot of old lace and linen that Mollie thought might have been a dowry. Chris went on to open the next while she rummaged a bit. The lace was beautiful. They went through several boxes this way, finding junk, farm medicines and even old toys.

'You could sell all this for a fortune, I'm sure!'

Chris heaved open the largest, and they finally found more documents than they could ever have dreamed. They poured over them but couldn't really make head nor tail of them.

'I guess we need to give this lot to the experts, so they can truly blacken my family,' said Chris with the first smile for a long time. Mollie smiled back in relief. He really wasn't that bad. There was one box left, which looked newer than the others. He raised his eyebrow. As Mollie nodded, he opened it, but this was quite different. It was filled with recent papers, going back over the last twenty or so years, but underneath was a series of books. Chris picked one up and opened it and drew a gasp.

'It seems my mother kept a diary.' He rummaged some more. 'This one here is the year they died. I wonder why it's here, not in the study?' Mollie could see he was welling up.

'Well, you must read them. There may be some answers about the accident and all the stuff from when you were a kid. You take that downstairs and I'll bring the old documents. I'll put them in this crate, so we don't damage them.'

He followed her silently down the stairs, shaken to his core. It was like waking the dead to see his mother's familiar handwriting all over again. Once in the sitting room, he shut the door firmly on Mollie and went to sort through. It was so personal, as if he was intruding. But there must be some answers. She had kept the diaries from when she had married, but he really didn't want to know all that; he went to the year of his birth. First, there were bits about being sick, then the due date, then a big gap which re-started a couple of weeks after he was born.

It's been so long since I've had the time or energy to write here, but I must ease my aching heart. Writing this down, I hope helps me feel better. The labour was just as bad as I thought it would be, but at least we got there in time for the epidural. Tony was so funny he didn't know what to do and hid in the corner until I demanded he come and hold my hand. I didn't expect to know when to push, because I couldn't feel anything, but the monitor and my body told me I needed to, and we yelled for the midwife. They were suddenly all there, and equally suddenly it was all over. I'm so glad I couldn't feel it, it was worse than a bad bout of constipation! My blood covered, slimy, but beautiful little son! We could see he was blonde like Tony and we had a quick cuddle before they whisked him off for all the tests and weighing things; it seemed like forever. They gave him back to us all wrapped up, and we just gazed and gazed at him, those clear blue eyes that looked as if he knew us already. I fed him while they stitched me up after the afterbirth came away, that made me feel like one of the cows! He latched on really well and we were soon trundled away to the ward. Tony was like a cat with two heads; he was calling everyone, and he was so proud. I just felt so tired. I bundled him off to the pub. It was so odd to see it was only 5 in the evening; it felt as if I had been taken to another world. I soon fell asleep, and when I woke it was dark, but there he was beside me and I picked him up and unwrapped him. He was perfect. I was lucky that there was no one in that little ward, as they took him away for the first night, so I slept as I have never done, and only woke for breakfast. Tony had been in and there was a huge bunch of flowers, such a heavenly scent.

I can't bear to write the next bit, but I must. All was lovely until the paediatrician came around the next day, to give us the all clear to go home. This really beaky guy turned up with a clique of students and they all sort of barged in; didn't ask if we wanted them. Then, in a really patronising voice, as if talking to a couple of idiots, he informed us that our little Chris was Hermaphrodite. He said these awful words that keep coming back to haunt me. Congenital adrenal hyperplasia. I can't bear to write it all down. My boy may be a boy, he may be a girl, he may be one or the other. The doctor then went on to say they may need to operate to correct things, and my baby may need hormones and treatment. I still can't get my head around it. But I screamed 'No, you're not touching him! You're not going to mutilate him, and it may be wrong later.' I had no idea where these words were coming from, but I got more and more hysterical as the doctor kept on insisting this was the right thing, and he knew best. Finally, Tony exploded, too, and threw them out of the room, with the doctor and his gang of cronies who were still complaining and saying they would be back when I had calmed down and saw sense.

Then, as is if from heaven, came a tap on the door, and there was Reverend Jones. We were both sobbing like a couple of toddlers after a tantrum and told him all about it. He let us calm down, and then he picked Chris up and prayed over him. He claimed healing and protection for him through the years and a happy long life. Then he sat down on the chair with Chris and waited for us to regain our calm completely. Then he looked at us and smiled. His words are engraved on my heart.

'I, too, was born like this, and I can only think God sent me here to protect Chris from what they did to me. I was born nearer a girl, but they decided I was more boy. I've had surgery and treatments all my life, until I was old enough to call a halt. Then before I was completely lost, I had my calling. I will fight with you for your son; I will be at your side every step of the way. We will keep him safe to be what he will be.'

Chris put the diary down. Hermaphrodite, inbetweenie, boy girl, weird, tomboy, ladyboy, transvestite, cross dresser, gay, nance, dike, pouff, Nancy boy. Everyone and none of these applied to him. It hurt, but it explained everything. Before he could change his mind, he picked up the phone and called Sandy and arranged to meet him in Southampton. Sandy would know this world. He would help him make sense of it and direct him where things had changed so much since he was born, where now, he could see a way forward. Until then, he was going to read the intervening years and see what had happened. He had no memory of hospitals, no scars; it seemed that they had won, and he had an even greater debt than before to his parents.

SEVENTEEN

Mollie left Chris alone. She guessed these diaries would help him resolve the inner conflicts. Now she concentrated on herself. She milked and then checked the calves. They were getting bigger by the minute and she really wondered why they were still here but wasn't going to take the decision herself. With their big eyes and ever-present tongue probe, they were nearly as cute as a foal. It gave her a huge inner joy to see them with their mums and that wonderful bond. It would be fun to have some cows of her own and run a herd on her own ideas. She hadn't had the chance to talk to Chris about her master plan, but she was sure he would think it a good one. Musing on this, she went in and had a bath and did her hair, which was in extra frizz mode, but what the heck, she wasn't out on a date to charm anyone! Still, she couldn't help thinking that under other circumstances, firstly, he would never have given her a look, and second, he was quite a good looking bloke, which was made worse by the contrast with Chris's blonde pinkness and thinness. Looking in the mirror, she decided that she wouldn't bother with makeup. He wasn't going to get anything gilded. Now ready, she banged on the sitting room door and Chris grunted a reply. So long as he knew she was gone. He had promised to keep his mobile on, so if she had an emergency, he would come and beat James up if needed.

The hotel certainly looked glamorous, lit up with fairy lights and with a large welcoming foyer. She was just going to the reception desk when James materialised. He certainly washed up well. Not as thin as Chris, he was darkly good looking. In that split second, she took a hold of herself. He had used her once and probably would again. He reached to formally shake her hand, but kept hold of it.

'The table is ready, but would you like a drink first?' He smiled what seemed to be the first genuine smile, and to her annoyance, it suited him.

'No thanks, let's just go in.' She tried a neutral smile, if that were possible. Still holding her hand, he led her in, and she didn't have the courage to wrest it away. It wasn't unpleasant, but she felt just a little trapped. However, they were soon being ushered to a little corner table that looked out into the spot lit grounds. There was a small fountain playing, and Mollie tried to resist a giggle but couldn't. James raised an eyebrow.

'Let us in on it?'

'It's just such a cliché here, the little table for two, the fountain and the waiters hovering. Can't take it seriously.'

'Well, we don't have to stay here.'

'No, no. Please just allow me my titter.' He had cleverly wrong-footed her. She was saved by the waiter arriving with the menus and from there it was all fairly straightforward, ordering food and making small talk about what they liked, with Mollie making it clear she was on the fruit juice. It was easy, too, over the starters; then James took over the conversation.

'I'm so glad you came. I really wanted to make a clear apology for all that happened when I stayed with you. I don't like the idea of someone having the wrong opinion of me.' Mollie snorted inwardly; she hoped this was going to be good.

'You may know that I'm a thriller writer, and a couple of my books are films... Ritual Death, Mad Monkey?' Mollie shook her head; they sounded awful.

'Well, writing is my career and passion. I got into it after I left Eton, and I make a living from it. My parents are Lord and Lady Cord-Rice, and we own Beamington castle?' Again, she couldn't help him on that; she hoped he was getting frustrated that she was totally unimpressed.

'Anyway, I suppose I come from a privileged background and with that come things such as accepted drinking and drug taking. I started at school and never gave up on it. My social scene took it as normal and I never really gave it serious thought. It was when I was writing the last book that I had a serious bust-up with the parents, and they threw me out. My girlfriend walked out, too, and I had to get the book finished for a deadline. I had my publisher breathing down my neck. Then I met your wonderful mother at a party, and she gave me the opportunity to use the cottage to write in peace.' If only he knew. Two of a kind.

'When I arrived at your place, I was partially out of my head the whole time. I took things when I was writing and when I wasn't. This was why I lost the picture. It was only when I took the book to my publisher and she claimed it was such complete gobbledegook that I realised I had to change. I rushed around the world a bit, then got in re-hab in the USA. They sorted me out and I'm back on the straight and narrow. I remembered where the picture was, and I'm sorry for giving you all the hassle.' He sat back and smiled complacently.

'So, you don't remember much else? Like when my dog was in season and you drove down to the stables and caused an accident which put my boss in hospital and this eventually led to me losing my job? Don't even remember the night you finished the book and came around with a bottle of champagne?'

'Er, no. Tell me exactly what.' He looked mortified as Mollie gave him the complete story in no uncertain terms and with no forgiveness.

'Oh, Lord, I have no memory of this at all. I'm really, really sorry. That's the trouble with drugs; they make you into a user of people and a taker, too. I don't know how to make it up to you.' Inside he was gloating at his perfect performance.

'You don't have to. We don't have a relationship. We will probably never meet again. I'm just glad that I've had a chance to tell you exactly what I think of you! And as for sending that tarty dress! What do you think I am, really, some sort of cheap lay to keep you occupied? Were you hoping for a repeat performance of that night? I feel sorry for you.'

At that moment, the main course arrived, and in the hostile silence, Mollie tucked in. She was going to have her meal; she was hungry, and he was paying. James watched Mollie eat; no finesse there, then.

'Look, I can only repeat my apology. I really don't know how to make it up to you. Can I make up some of the lost wages?'

'No, I'm financially independent, thank you.'

'Then, what then? how do I make you forgive me?'

'You need my forgiveness? Why, just so your conscience is satisfied and you can walk away thinking that after all, you're a great bloke?'

'No, it's not that. I just want to make amends. I'm not the person I want to be yet, but I'm not what I was. I've discovered what it is to be hurt and to hurt, whereas I've been totally impervious before. It would really help me if we could form some sort of armed neutrality, so I could walk away knowing that some of the wounds have been healed. Then I could look on myself as less of a user as you say, and that there may be some hope for me as a person. I might then have a chance of one day forming a normal sort of relationship and life. Could we not just take a step back to the day when I turned up on your front door and start again?'

Mollie looked at him as she chewed on a slightly tough piece of steak. It sounded quite reasonable and if he really had no memory of these things, how could she go on being so antagonistic? It would put her as a worse person than he was. She enjoyed his dark chocolate voice and it was quite nice to have him actually begging. She paused over another mouthful.

'How would you see this armed neutrality? I'm not about to be your girlfriend, so just what are you expecting?'

'I don't really know!' His sudden smile was disarming. 'But maybe we could just meet and chat a couple of times. I'll only be here for a couple more weeks; then I have to get back to work on the next book.'

'I'll concede a dog walk or two, if that would do? Mud, wellies, dogs, on my terms, and maybe the horses and cows, too.'

'That sounds great.' He did that smile again. It could almost turn her knees if she let them. 'I did spend a lot of time as a kid on the estate with the gun dogs getting into all sorts of trouble.' Oh, no, more mucky boots. He battened down on his emotions.

Mollie managed a smile as she wondered if she would bother training Mutantmutt not to jump at the back of his legs or not. The rest of the meal was pleasant, as James took over the conversation with anecdotes about his writing life and the famous people he had met when he could remember that was. It was nearly midnight when Mollie got into her car, unmolested and happier. She waved as she pulled away. James made his way to his room where he had a bottle of something nice waiting. He would try those new little pills he had picked up in a night club. He really had done a great job this time. He hadn't lost his touch as the arch manipulator. He had fooled all those shrinks in rehab, and he'd got her, too. It would only be a matter of time before he won the little fool over. Get her in a soppy frame of mind; then he would walk. Revenge for losing his picture and the trouble with the police. Game, set and match.

Chris was also preparing for a sort of date, although he really hoped it would just be a chat where he could get some answers for all his dilemmas. He thrust to the back of his mind all that was troubling him and concentrated on the now. He showered, put on clean jeans and shirt, hoping that if this was good enough for the pub, it would do for a music bar in Southampton. He found the car park and station easily; after all, it was signposted from everywhere. He could see and hear the club from where he had parked. The men he saw going in were just blokes, no drag queens or men in heavy make-up. Smart yes. At that thought, he shifted a bit uneasily in his seat. He was half an hour early. If he could pluck up courage, he would go on in. He and Sandy had swapped photos and he was a quite distinct person, over six foot, with fair, sandy hair. It was a nickname. His real name was Peter. He would arrive in his van, which had his firm's name plastered all over it, so there definitely would be no problem. Chris guessed that his mud splattered truck would also be a giveaway.

His phone bleeped with a text. Sandy was running half an hour late and suggested they meet inside, even saying which table to sit in as the place should be free. He even asked Chris to order him his meal, as the service was always a bit slow. This gave Chris the courage to go in. It wasn't unlike any other club that he had been to. The band was setting up, and there were just a few people at the bar. He found the seat that Sandy had recommended, ordered food and drinks, then hid behind his mobile as he saw several other people doing. The door swung open and in rushed a group of about twenty men, probably on a hen/stag night, as they were wearing pink tiaras and t-shirts and one had bride written on his. They had clearly been to several places before, as the smell of alcohol wafted in with them. They put the juke box on and proceeded to party.

Chris didn't know what to do. He was scared, as it wasn't like a do from the Young Farmers where he knew them all and exactly what they would get up to. He'd even been a ringleader on the odd occasion. He texted Sandy that things had got lively and how long would he be? If he hadn't ordered food, he would have got back into the truck and waited. He felt very, very, trapped. Then things got worse as some of the men went to the tables and pulled people to their feet to dance with them, ignoring any protestations. When a huge bulk of a man stood in front of Chris with a big grin and a waving magic wand, he knew he had no option but to get up and join in...

Mollie drove home in a strange mood. Half of her thought that she had caved in too easily. The other half argued that a couple of dog walks wouldn't hurt; she could always push him into the mud with Mutantmutt's help. She didn't really want a relationship with him, but she wanted to sort her life out and give it some meaning. That didn't entail another relationship that would go nowhere, and she would be hurt again. It could be she was more like her mother than she thought if she could be so determined not to be distracted from her plan. She would talk to Chris soon, and try to go on with talking him out of his rut. She saw the tractor was where he had abandoned it in the field.

The full moon was coming out as she crossed the yard and she could hear one of the cows lowing in the barn. Interested to see what they were getting up to under cover of darkness, she went in to watch them in the pale light. The claves were prancing about, and Mollie wanted to giggle. Like foals, they could always play the fool. There was an unfamiliar noise in the background that she couldn't quite make out: it wasn't the cows, so she went in. She could now see there was a heap of something in the middle. Mystified, she got closer and the moaning got louder. Her alarm bells went off. Was this some trick from the kids in the village? Was she about to be mugged? She got her mobile out and switched the torch on and shone the beam into the blood-smeared face of Chris.

EIGHTEEN

His eyes opened, and he spoke in a hoarse whisper. 'No ambulances. No hospital. Call Dr Wright in the village. Now help me up.' At which point he passed out. Mollie ran, switched the barn light on and shoved the cows out into the yard. She didn't really know what to do, so she went back to his stricken form. He was breathing, but his limbs were twisted, his clothes torn. How was she ever going to lift him? Some dim memory of a first aid course kicked in. She knew she mustn't move him as she didn't know the injuries, but surely he should be in the recovery position? And kept warm. She rushed off and found the old horse blankets in the tack room and covered him over. She then reached for her mobile for the telephone number for the doctor. There seemed to be no one practising under this name in the village. Maybe he was retired, so she just typed in the name. Bingo!

'Hello, is that Dr Wright, who used to be the village doctor? I'm at Grey's farm and Chris has had a terrible accident, but he's refusing to let me ring the ambulance. He asked for you. Oh, please, can you come and help?'

There was a sigh at the end of the line. 'It seems I'll never be able to retire. I'm on my way, where will I find you?'

She was swiftly gone, and Mollie still didn't know what to do. Then something of her childhood kicked in and she began to pray and to pray hard, using some of the old familiar words but also a primaeval call for help. Then she heard the sound of a car coming into the yard. That was a quick answer. She went out and found not an old doctor, but a young bloke in a plumber's van.

'Can you help me? I'm looking for Chris Brown. I was supposed to meet him this evening in Southampton, but things went wrong.'

Mollie was eyeing his clothes and hands to see if they were bloodstained.

'And you are who?' she asked aggressively.

'Sandy. We've been chatting online for a while and we were meeting for the first time. So this is the right place? Where is he?'

Sandy was quite tall and tried to peer around Mollie, who was trying to block him. The dogs heard their voices from the house and began a peal of angry barking.

'How did you find this place? He obviously wouldn't have told you.'

'Phonebook, old school. Look, where is he? I'm sure something terrible has happened and I need to find him. Is he here?' His voice was rising with panic, and Mollie had to make a quick decision.

'I'll have to trust you. I have your registration number and phone from the van if not. I've just found him in the barn. He's been beaten up badly and is unconscious. I'm waiting for the doctor. He refused the ambulance before he blacked out.'

'Can I see him? This is all my fault.

Mollie led the way in just as another car swung into the yard. Its entrance scared the cows who began to misbehave. Mollie saw no other option but to push them out into the field with the others to get them out of the way. As she slammed the gate, the doctor was getting her bag out of the boot. Sandy was just standing as she had left him.

'Now what has happened? is it the tractor again?'

'No, it looks like he has been beaten up. I've just found him in the barn. He was conscious, but now he's out cold.'

The doctor strode off, obviously familiar with the place. Chris hadn't moved. Without a word, she threw off the rugs and bent to her knees and examined him. At the disturbance, Chris moaned and come to, but he was incoherent. The doctor checked every limb, his chest and head.

'Turn your backs,' she barked. Then after a couple of minutes, 'Right, there's no broken bones, just bruising and cuts. We need to get him indoors and clean him up; then I might have to insist on an ambulance. Do you have an old gate or door we could use?' She was addressing Sandy.

'I live here. This is just a friend. There's a door in the yard. Sandy, make yourself useful,' Mollie now barked and he leapt to help. Together, the three of them gently lifted Chris onto the base and tied him gently so he wouldn't slip. Sandy's strength was a godsend. Mollie knew she wouldn't have managed without him. She yelled at the dogs to be quiet and at the first opportunity, shut them out. They took Chris into the kitchen and put him on the table.

'Not the first time I've done this, but not under these circumstances. I will want a full explanation.' Dr Wright glared at them. 'Now, we'll need water to clean him, fresh clothes eventually. Young man, get my bag from the barn.'

Chris was now getting restless, but not yet awake.

'Hey, it's OK. The doctor is here; we've got you safe.' Mollie took his hand, and it seemed to help. There was no time for sentiment or nausea as Chris' wounds were stitched and bound. The work was in silence. His clothes were cut away, he had wounds all over his body and his eyes were swelling with bruising. But the worst was around his genitals and Mollie turned her face away.

'Packs of frozen veg?' They were swiftly found, and the doctor took the packs and bound them onto his groin. She put Chris on a makeshift drip and filled him with various injections.

'You're lucky that I've just been doing work as a locum, or I wouldn't have had all this gear. Now we get him into bed. I don't suppose the one in the living room is a sofa bed?' Mollie nodded and rushed off to make it up with fresh linen. Then between them, cradling him like a large baby, they got him onto the bed and laid him gently down.

'Now get the heating on, and we'll leave him; he's sedated.'

In the kitchen, they faced the doctor's fury.

'You better have a good explanation for this, or I will have him in hospital and call the police. '

'I was out this evening. I found him when I checked the calves. He was on his computer when I left.' They both turned and looked at Sandy, who sank to a chair.

'This is all my fault. We have been talking on a gay website for a while and he suddenly rang me this evening and asked to meet up; something was troubling him. We agreed to meet at Shirly's in town, but I got held up on a job. He had arrived early, so he went in and ordered some meals for us. Then my job took even longer, and I didn't get there for another hour. The place was deserted and the band was packing up. Apparently, a hen do had been in and caused a riot, wrecking the band's equipment and breaking things. When the gang was threatened with the police, they took off, taking several people with them, and from the description, Chris was with them.'

'Hen do, as in a gay do, all blokes?' butted in the doctor. Sandy nodded.

'I drove all around the city. I tried all the other bars, but nothing. Then someone said they had seen a coach party arrive, so maybe they had gone away in this. So, I thought maybe Chris had gone home. I knew he had an old truck; we had joked about it. It was nowhere in any of the car parks.

His mobile was going straight to answerphone. I found his address and came straight over.'

'If you two are telling the truth, which seems likely, then we will probably not find these men without the help of the police, who could track them down on CCTV. But in the light of the nature of the attack, I can see why Chris was so adamant. Heavens, woman, put the kettle on; I'm exhausted.' She slumped on a chair. 'You! Go and check on him.'

Sandy scuttled off. Mollie soon put steaming mugs on the table and also the bottle of whiskey.

'He seems more relaxed,' reported Sandy.

'I should hope so, too, with all the dope I've pumped into him. Do either of you know anything of his childhood?'

'I know he was home-schooled and his parents were killed in a car accident a few years ago.' Mollie ventured.

'Well, I will tell you this. Chris was born what some would call a hermaphrodite, but what we now call intersex. His parents and the Rev Jones fought battles with the social services before they lost interest. They wanted to give him surgery and other treatments. But his parents were maybe ahead of their time and refused. He grew up as they said he was and it seems they were right to do so.'

'He said to me he had found out something today and really needed to chat with a bloke about it. Sorry, Mollie, isn't it?'

She nodded. 'We found his mother's diaries yesterday. So maybe that was it. Do you think he didn't know? That's incredible.'

'It could be so. He was kept out of all the cases and highly protected.'

'That makes a lot of sense. So this has a bearing on the attack?'

'Undoubtedly. The way he has been bruised and cut in his groin smacks of a systematic beating.'

Sandy groaned. 'I never had any idea. I'm plain gay, so I don't understand any of this. How anyone could do this to someone under any circumstances is unbelievable.'

'Well, it's happened, and I will try to continue to protect him as I did in his childhood.'

'Does the entire village know?'

'I would like to think not; his parents were so careful and were happy to be branded nuts to home school because it was their problem.'

Sandy began to sob.

'Look, mate, you will be needed at this time, as you seem to be his only contact. If you aren't prepared to hang around and support him in his recovery, then you better take off now before he even knows that you were here. And if you do, you don't keep on whining at it being all your fault; that won't help either. Be a man for want of a better word and be there. And you, young lady, you will have to run this place for him. It's a big farm, but at least it's autumn, not harvest time. I will spread the word that it's a cattle incident. Did I see some calves? They always cause trouble.'

She reached for the whiskey and poured them all a large jot. 'I have lived in Hazeley all my life, and it's my work. I can't give up helping the people I have seen into the world. Any indiscretion on the part of either of you and you will have me to contend with. Is that clear?'

'No!' said Mollie. 'We're not going to say it was the cattle. If we get into lying, we'll make things worse. All anyone needs to know is that he's been beaten up in a club in Southampton. No one ever need know any more.'

The doctor looked at her with some respect. 'That's agreed, then. I will be back in the morning. The fact that I am up here will have the Hazeley gossip phone in overdrive by mid morning, so be prepared for phone calls and nosiness.'

They nodded dumbly.

'He will be fine until the morning. I'll check that drip and we can take the icepacks off now. One of you will sit with him until I return and if he does wake and shows signs of distress, give him one of these. If they don't work, call me.' She seemed to turn the gruff off. 'You two are all he's got.'

She stood, stretched, picked up her bag and left. Mollie and Sandy looked at each other. Mollie poured another drink.

'Are you going to be around for him? He's really no more than a complete stranger to you.'

'I don't know. I have a full day's work ahead of me tomorrow, and I can't see how I can get out of it, being my own boss, that is. But I can be here as soon as I finish and be here for the weekend. During that time I can check my appointment books, and maybe we'll have an idea of how he is. What is puzzling me is how he ever managed to drive back.'

'I know, we'll have to look for his truck in daylight.' Mollie looked at her watch. 'I have to milk in two hours. I'll have to be here all tomorrow on my own, so could I have a kip if you sit with him?'

'I'll try to keep awake.'

'Are you okay with dogs?' He nodded, so she let them in. Her two weren't bothered, but Rex had to sit and look pathetic by the sitting room door. Mollie couldn't be doing with that, so she went upstairs, calling the dogs with her, but Rex didn't budge. She set the alarm and fell immediately into a deep sleep before her mind took over. Waking was like being washed in cold water as it all came back. She struggled into her working gear and slid downstairs, hoping it was all a bad dream.

What was left of his clothes were all over the kitchen and discarded medical packs all over the floor. She swept them all up and put them onto the fire and lit it. She let the dogs out and even Rex went, then she washed down the table. She couldn't put it off any longer and peered into the sitting room. Sandy was lying prone next to Chris, fast asleep, but was holding his hand. Chris's face was more swollen than before, the bruising setting in, but he was breathing peacefully and rhythmically. She stepped over Sandy and removed the drip from Chris. Not a problem as she had done this with horses in the past. Neither moved. She would leave them and go milk.

NINETEEN

Mollie was expecting there to be problems milking, but to her surprise, the situation was almost laughable. The girls were all lined up to come in, including Ziggy and Queenie, and the calves were with them. She let them into the parlour and, like it was an ordinary day, they slotted into their places; didn't kick or shove. The only difference was the calves ran around and each cow lowed after them as if they were their own. She didn't bother with the two real mums, as they were now having all their output drunk. She let them all out with a sense of relief. It could have been a real problem if there had been protective mums. But no, they ambled away, each cow mothering a calf when it got near. This soothed Mollie's weeping heart.

She wasn't in love with Chris, but he was her dearest friend; he was all she had at the moment. He didn't deserve such a thing. The doctor's revelations made sense to her, making all his little oddnesses clear and Chris just being Chris kicking into place. She felt herself welling up with sorrow for him, but the sun was coming over the hill, and she knew Sandy would have to leave. She left the cows and saw the tractor still on the hill where

Chris had left it. She would have to find someone to finish the job and soon.

Back inside, she found Sandy blearily putting the kettle on. She made him sit and got him some breakfast. They swopped numbers, and he was soon on his way. Taking a mug of coffee, Mollie went into the sitting room. This time she let the dogs in; they needed to see him too. They sniffed, but she didn't let them touch, and they all seemed to register the situation as they all went and lay down on the dog bed without a growl or altercation. As quietly as she could, she pulled up the armchair and sat beside him. Looking at her phone, she saw two messages from James, who she had conceded to unblock, but that seemed another lifetime ago and she didn't bother to read them. She swiftly texted Joanna, saying they had found the documents but wouldn't be able to bring them over for a couple of days; hopefully that would mean no visits. When would that doctor arrive? Like the dogs, she soon dozed off, too, and was woken by the doctor walking into the room. 'He must be OK' was Mollie's first thought as the dogs just looked, wagged their tales a bit and went back to bed.

'How's he been, then?'

'Sandy says he was a little restless, but he went back to sleep. He hasn't moved, really.'

The doctor was now doing the doctor things of blood pressure and temperature.

'How did I get here?' asked Chris in a hoarse

voice.

'I found you in the barn. Doctor Wright has treated you; no hospital, like you said.'

'Have you milked? What's the time?'

'All's done and it's just after nine.'

'I must finish the sowing.' Chris tried to rise, but with a gasp of pain, sank back down again and moaned. 'I can't see properly.'

'You've got two massive shiners, Chris. Can you remember last night?' He struggled to open his mouth now, so Mollie got him some water. With shaking hands, he took the glass and drank.

'I was waiting for this guy, Sandy, and he was delayed. So, I went into the club and ordered the meal. Then this hen night came in and took over the place. I found myself being pulled into it. Heavens knows what they put in my drink. The next thing I knew was being outside and we were by the sea. They were all taking their clothes off and when I refused, they were taking them off me. I don't know why they hated me. They laughed and called me a freak, and then they hit me...' He sank back into the pillow.

'All I can hear are the words they used, mutant, freak, freak, freak. Then I blacked out. When I woke up, I was alone on the beach. I found my clothes and walked back to the car park. I knew the beach from a school trip. Then I drove home. I don't remember any more, except the whole time, I felt there was someone with me, someone who had his arm around me all the time and helped me into the truck and made sure I took the right turnings. He cradled me in the straw until you found me.'

'There wasn't anyone there when I found you.'

'There was.' In his insistence, he struggled.

'It's all right, Chris. Maybe they had just gone. Where is your truck?'

'Just behind the stables.'

'Mollie, I think you should go and check that while I see to Chris.'

She obeyed the authority and realised that her presence wasn't wanted. The truck was there, just as he had said, but with blood all over the seats. If there had been someone else there, there was no sign of it. Perhaps Chris was just hallucinating. His keys were still in it, so she took them. Crossing the yard, she found Joanna at the field gate looking at the calves.

'I'm sorry. When I got your text, I had to divert my dog walk to collect them... What's up, Mollie? You look like you've seen a ghost. Why is Dr Wright here? I saw her car; has something happened?'

Joanna's care broke Mollie, and she sat on the wet grass and told Joanna the story, well, the official version with tears flooding down her cheeks. 'It's all so awful and he wasn't that happy at the moment anyway. And now I have to run the farm, and I really don't have a clue how to do it. I've never driven a tractor!'

Joanna put her arm around her. 'I think

there will be plenty of help. At times like this, Hazeley people pull together. I'll activate the bush telegraph and see what we can do. No chance of the documents though?' They both grinned and went in to fetch the box. Of course, the dogs were overjoyed to see them, so they let them all out into the fields for a run. Even Rex was up for a tussle.

'I won't be able to come in for a while either. I hate to let you down, but I need to be here for him.'

'If things do get bad, I'll ask Chloe to come up earlier, so don't worry. Your job will remain open. Would you like me to pray for you?'

Mollie shrank back. No, she wasn't having anything from a God who could allow this. 'Er, no, that's fine, just wait here and I'll fetch the box.'

Joanna watched Mollie inwardly ranting at herself; that really was bad timing, but she could pray now.

Dr Wright was washing her hands when Mollie returned to the house. 'He's doing better than expected. I think we got to him in good time, and in daylight everything looks better. I've stitched two cuts I missed. What was a hen party doing with knives?' She shook her head. 'You will need to keep a close eye on him and encourage him to move as much as he can. Plenty of tea and coffee. Feed him up; he's much too thin, anyway. Encourage him to walk to the loo, but if not, I'm sure there's a pot somewhere that can be used. Just check there's no blood in it. Where's that bloke?'

'He's had to go to work, but will be here in the evening, and for the weekend.'

'Well, we might not need him so urgently, but Chris may need a bloke for help with some things.' Mollie didn't want to know. 'I'll pop by this evening. There are more tablets over there, but don't leave any medication in the room with him. He might not remember what he's taken. It would be so much easier in the hospital, but he's as stubborn as ever. Now, how are you coping?'

'I'll be fine. I can manage the cows. Joanna has said that she will organise some help with the tractor, as I can't drive one.'

'Good, good. I'll pop back this evening.' And she swung out. Mollie made a pot of tea and bacon sandwiches, then marched in to Chris. He was now semi-sitting. She wanted to engulf him in a hug but knew that would hurt.

'Breakfast! I've orders to feed you up.'

He looked at her through slitted eyes. 'You must think I'm a right prat! Has she told you all the gory details?'

'Enough, but I love you anyway,' she said roguishly, then was aware that probably wasn't the right thing. 'I'm here for you 24/7. I will do everything you need. You are not a prat. Don't ever think you are in any way at fault about this. If you do, I will slap you. Got it?'

He almost grinned. 'Give me food, but I might need a straw with the tea. My lips are swollen, too.'

To her relief, he managed both sandwiches and

a couple of mugs of tea. Then he slumped back. 'I'm stuffed. I might need to doze; the pills are great. But put the TV on and give me the buttons.' Mollie did so. Then the dogs were barking outside.

'No visitors!' Chris yelped.' Pull the curtains, too. I don't want anyone peeping. Lock the front door.'

When Mollie got to the yard, she found a rather large bloke standing outside, stroking the dogs. 'I-er-um- got a call from Joanna. She says Chris has had a pounding at a pub and needs some help. I'm Gary from Hazeley Manor Farm.'

'Oh, please.' Relief washed over Mollie as she remembered Chris mentioning him. 'He's not seeing anyone just yet; it was only last night, but I'm Mollie, his housemate.' She put out her hand and had it engulfed in a huge rough one. 'He was halfway through sowing the higher field yesterday and had to stop. If you could finish that... and I need some more hay and silage for the feeding aisle in the parlour. If you could do that, it would really help.'

'No sweat. Are the keys in the tractor?' He strode off and Mollie felt supported. This wasn't the last visit of the day. When Andy came to collect the milk, he offered to do some of the milking shifts, which was a real relief, as Mollie was starting to feel tired. Then it seemed Joanna had called the church and people started popping by with ready cooked meals and offers of shopping trips. She felt overwhelmed. What with checking on Chris, helping Gary with the jobs and then milking, she was definitely flagging. But Gary was a gentle helper and she found him easy to work with. As it was growing dark, he drove away with a pledge of just a phone call if she needed anything else. Sandy arrived with an overnight bag and she got him up to date with the day's events. He had the idea of putting a sign on the doors saying thanks and please leave stuff as Chris was resting but leave a number so we can thank you. After milking, they locked and barred the doors. Sandy had hung back from going in, as it was entirely possible that Chris wouldn't know who he was. Mollie had to go in with him.

'Chris, there's someone to see you.' Again, he jumped and appeared to pull into himself.

'Oh, mate, I'm so sorry. I'm Sandy and this is all my fault.'

Mollie groaned inwardly; just what the doctor had told him not to say. But Chris was peering at him and it looked like a smile. 'It's okay. I know you were here last night. You know all that happened and it was just one of those things. I bear no grudge. Mollie, put the kettle on; I need to talk to him.'

She never found out what their conversation was about, as the doorbell rang and with a groan, she went to see who it was. Maybe she had locked the doctor out. And she groaned again when she saw who it was. James stood at the door with the regulation bunch of flowers and chocolates. So that was what all the texts had been about.

'Look, James, I'm really sorry. There's been an accident and Chris has been injured. I really don't have time for this; I haven't stopped all day. I'm exhausted.'

A shout came from Sandy in the sitting room. 'Who is it?'

'James, to take me out.' She was aware that she was holding him out.

'Chris says go out and take a break.'

James pushed himself in. 'Come on, it's only a meal at the village pub. You look like you could do with a drink.' He was looking around for the dogs.

Mollie suddenly wanted to laugh. 'They're in the kitchen. Can I come like this?' She was in old jeans and a smeared sweatshirt.

'You're fine!' That really surprised her, as he was in smart corduroys and sweater.

'But please, not the village pub. Somewhere away from Hazeley. They'll all be asking questions and I've had enough today.' She was just realising that she had fed everyone but herself.

'Your wish is my command.' He smiled a real grin that Mollie had never seen before, and he swept her out into his car. Mollie now discovered a new James. He was courteous, led the conversation and listened with interest to her story. She was nevertheless careful to tell him the edited version; she wasn't ready to put her full trust in him yet. The food was delicious and Mollie ate and drank well, feeling the weight lifting from her. But before long, her head was begging to droop, and James took her home. At the door, he kissed her on the top of her head and sent her indoors with a changing opinion of the former rat. She popped her head around the sitting room door. Chris was asleep, Sandy was asleep on the dog sofa, and the dogs were asleep around him. She'd forgotten to tell him about the spare room.

James drove away, chucking to himself. He really should have been an actor. Whatever the truth of the tale, and he was sure she hadn't told him everything, that twit's accident had given him the opening he had thought would take much longer. Brilliant, he was getting near the goal.

In the next few weeks, as Chris's body recovered, a small support team grew around him that began to be bound by friendship. Sandy popped over and chatted with Chris, but from what Mollie could see and Chris let slip, it was mates chat, a first genuine friendship. Gary and Andy helped her with the cows, and then Chris, as he got out and about. James took Mollie on dates, but it never got on any further; it was as if he was keeping himself deliberately back and this was arousing her interest in him. Then he suddenly disappeared on a book signing tour without a further word. Autumn was becoming winter and Joanna was the size of a small battleship, Mollie helping her more and more in the house. Dr Wright had talked a local physiotherapist into helping Chris get his muscles working again around the scars. No one mentioned his deeper scars; while Chris' body was healing, his mind wasn't. He spent a lot of time re-reading his mother's diaries and other papers he found in the loft, and always on the internet, but he wouldn't talk about it.

Then Chloe arrived.

TWENTY

Sunday lunch was becoming a regular thing. Mollie in her efforts to build Chris up had taken to cooking a huge roast, and the others sort of got involved, too. Afterwards, they would all sprawl in the sitting room and watch some stupid film. It was a gloomy, dull afternoon and they had just abandoned the washing up. Even the dogs were snoring in various positions around the room, as they had eaten their share too.

Chris was comfortable in the armchair he had commandeered for himself so that no one got too close. His body might be sated but his head was on the familiar treadmill that he never seemed to be able to get off. Why do they want to be near a freak? They would be better off without me. I could just pack my bags and walk; they would soon pull together and run this place better than I ever did. I'm a waste of space. Can't be a husband, father or even a lover. What use am I? Just as well, my parents aren't here to see what a useless prat I am. I wish those blokes had finished the job. On and on in similar vein while he tried to wear a smile on his face.

He was just starting the cycle again when there was an explosion of sound. Firstly, Joanna's dogs came rushing in looking for a game, then Joanna's bump, Joanna, Guy and a middle-aged woman with long flowing blonde hair and a hippie frock with wellies. Chloe. Diane's Mum. Joanna's he didn't know what. But he knew that he was in for yet another sympathetic chat and he really couldn't face one more. In the chaos of greetings and calming the dogs and introductions, he tried to slink away. No chance. As he got to his feet, he was engulfed in a famous Chloe hug, and for a microsecond, he relaxed into it. No, it was a false comfort and he pulled back.

'Chris, despite being in the wars, you're looking really well! You've been missed at the Manor, but I guess you've got an excuse!'

She tried that tack. Well, at least it was a bit original.

'Did they all come round and pray for you?'

'No, but it wasn't really needed; I'm getting on fine.'

He could see Joanna and Guy shrinking a bit as they overheard.

'That's a shame, but never mind. We could all get together some time. I'm here, ready for the new arrival. And you seem to have got lots of help while you're getting fit again. How wonderful!' She stood back from him and gave him a full-on eyeballing. He knew Chloe well from the house group at the Manor, so he did his best to give her a steady, assured, unblinking gaze back. He was fairly certain he had pulled it off, but she was so perceptive. It was scary. She smiled, and he heaved an inward sigh of relief.

'Now, this must be Mollie!' She had him by the arm and dragged Mollie away from a conversation about cows, which even Sandy seemed to find amusing, to get acquainted with her. Mollie stood up well to the interrogation. Chloe didn't use the thumbscrews this time, but he could sense her planning something when Mollie told her about her Catholic upbringing. He'd have to warn her about Chloe tactics later on. What was he thinking? Hadn't he been a keen member of the House Group for several years and had been to concerts and church meetings with them all? What had happened to the person heading for Bible college? It all seemed so far away. And irrelevant.

Once Mollie was released, there were cups of tea, cakes, and talk about so many things. Gary and Sandy got the treatment, too, but didn't seem to mind. It soon got dark and the guests took their leave, but Chris knew he wasn't off the hook by a long means and crept into the study for a bit of peace and quiet. He wasn't letting on to anyone what he was doing. Maybe they thought he was looking up doctors about his condition and getting help. But no, there was no point in that. He was following with a grim determination his own court cases, and he was trying to find Rev. Jones. He knew he owed him a big thank you for his childhood, and he was maybe the only person in the world who would understand the place where Chris was now. The Reverend had told Chris's mother about what he had suffered, so he must be now what Chris was, asexual. The beating had left him with little function, although he hadn't had much in the first place. At least the porn sites could pull him in no more. He went back to his computer and clicked on the search page.

Mollie was also relieved when the guests left. Chloe was a dear, but one of those freaky Christians that the nuns had always said were fanatics. Hopefully, talking about Catholicism would put her off the trail. The lads were now watching a football match and Chris was due to milk, so she tackled the washing up, luxuriating in the deep hot water from the aga kettle. So of course, as soon as she was up to her elbows in it, her phone rang.

'Hi, honey, I'm home!' It was James, sounding really upbeat. She really didn't want to see him tonight; she wanted to slob in front of the TV. 'I'm back early and wanted to celebrate with you! I've just cracked a new five-book deal with publishers in the USA. Boy, will I be in the money! Come for dinner with me? I've booked a table at the best restaurant in Winchester, so get your glad rags on. We're off; I'll be round in a half hour.' She was just trying to say no, but he had rung off.

She was trapped.

'Hey, guys, I'm off out tonight. If I finish the washing up, will you let the dogs out before you go? Chris might not remember.'

'Fine, we're actually going to drag him down to the pub after he's milked,' laughed Gary.

'I wish you the best of luck. If you can even get him out of the front door, I'll cook again next week.' They all exchanged conspiratorial smiles.

James arrived promptly and honked from the front yard. She guessed he wasn't going to get his smart gear muddy. She was greeted with a full-on smacker of a kiss that had her reeling, but she had plenty of time to recover, as he spent the entire time talking at her about his great success. When they parked, he threw an arm around her and she was whisked into one of the smartest places she'd ever seen. It just dripped money, expensive perfume, and had an air of aloofness. If James hadn't been propelling her, she would have run. Her clothes were plain and smart for once, but even so, she felt sloppy and dowdy.

'What do you think of this place, then?'

'It's quite wonderful, but I feel a bit out of my league.'

He grinned, 'Well let's just enjoy it. We don't need to ever come back if you don't like it.' He lifted up a huge menu. 'Do you want to tackle this, or shall I order for you?'

Something in Mollie rose; she wasn't going to be patronised, and she wasn't going to be found lacking. She snatched up her menu. For once, her endless language classes in school came into their own and she ordered swiftly, and with things she hoped would make him notice that she wasn't that dumb. But he was too immersed in the wine menu.

They settled into that limbo that comes before the food arrives. James suddenly looked into her eyes. 'So how have things been while I've been away? Is Chris getting better?' She wasn't going to let anyone in there.

'He's great, milking again, and the physiotherapy is working.'

'Did you get things sorted out with the solicitor?' Mollie had let slip about her parents and the deal in a moment she regretted, but he had given her the details of a 'good man' who wouldn't let them sneak in anything that might backfire. And they had, trying to put in a clause that would make Mollie responsible for any debts her parents left when they died. That had been so sneaky, and they had fought, saying it was only fair if she had all this money, but her man was tougher than theirs, and Mollie had won. All the money was gently accruing in her account, but she had never told James just how much, although he had tried to find out. Maybe it made him respect her a bit more.

'That's good. And what have you been up to yourself?' Good grief, he really was trying tonight, thought James, despite this sense of growing boredom.

'I've just been working with Joanna. They are still sorting out all the documents we found and helping in the house. Next year, when Chris is fully recovered, then I may move on.'

'Do you have any fixed plans?'

'Not really. I might stay put and buy myself a really good horse and get into eventing. I've always fancied that, and now I can.'

'Don't you want to do something new and exciting?'

'Everything is open.'

'I have something that might interest you. We seem to have got over our bad start.' He grinned roguishly. 'But, I was thinking that with the new book deal and all the film things that are going on, I could do with some help. We could do so much together. We haven't even really started this relationship; it seems to have been dogged with disaster. I really need someone, and you are just the most beautiful person I've ever met. I would love to take this relationship a whole step further, so we could work and live together, with all that entails. No commitments and you can set your own terms. I just would really like your company on this journey. We could begin by taking a short break to the US after Christmas and see how it goes. Imagine all the travelling, great places and people we would meet!'

Mollie didn't know what to say. She had felt he was just playing along, not really interested in her at all, although she had recently begun to hope it might take a new direction. He really seemed a different person to the one who had ruined things. But then again, how poor her life would have been if she had stayed as a slave for Liz.

'I know this sounds a cliché, but I am bowled over. James, let me think about this, but, really, really are you serious? I couldn't bear to be betrayed again.'

He took her hand in his and for the first time, she felt that pulse of excitement. He locked her with those brown eyes. She was saved by the arrival of the entrees. It didn't seem important what she was eating, because she couldn't taste it. It might have been cardboard.

They had just finished, and the plates were being taken away, and Mollie needed the loo. How unromantic. She had just made her way down the marble corridor and found that she had left her handbag behind. She needed her tampons, so she made her way back. As she turned the corner, she saw James reflected in a mirror on the opposite wall. He was sitting with what could only be called a smirk on his face. He took a sip and, looking at his phone, he smirked again, but this time it was nasty. He put the phone down and fished in his pocket. Out came a small tin, which Mollie remembered vaguely seeing when he had stayed with her. He opened it and took out a couple of pills. She could see them quite clearly. He washed them down with more wine, then looked complacently about him, then saw Mollie watching him in the mirror. She felt like she'd taken part in the ice bucket challenge all over again. His eyes bored into her. They were nothing but cold for a second, then it was if he consciously masked what was inside.

'Ah, Mollie, you were quick. Just got a bit of a headache'. But she knew enough, as she saw his pupils dilating.

'I won't grace you with what I think of you. Off drugs? Not a user anymore. You haven't changed in the slightest. At least I saw this before it was too late.' She wasn't going to let him speak. 'Goodbye, and if you show your face anywhere near me or the farm, I really will set the dogs on you.'

He sneered, but she snatched her handbag and left. Fortunately, as it was such a posh restaurant, they called her a taxi, with no questions asked. James hadn't followed her. Soon she was speeding home, with nothing but a tremendous sense of relief.

James took another swig. The pills really were kicking in. You lose some, you win some. The world was his oyster again; he didn't need to wait for that horse-faced bitch. Rats to the revenge, he had great things happening. He'd give that girl he had met on the plane a call. She looked the ironing type...

Mollie paid the cab and went through the double doors of the pub to be met with a wall of singing, smoke and fumes of alcohol. She stood completely in shock as she saw Gary, Sandy and Chris standing on a table, belting out I will survive to a karaoke machine. Then she began to laugh, a deep belly laugh that she hadn't had for years. Putting her bag under a seat, she leapt up and joined in, grabbing the mike from Chris. One more round in drunk verse and the song was over. There was a huge round of applause. The four of them jumped down. They were all absolutely rat arsed, wobbly and with huge grins on their faces. Mollie grabbed what was left of Chris's pint and knocked it back. 'You doing an encore??' They all looked at each other, but they had been beaten to it, as another gang had jumped on the table.

They swayed their way to a table, and Mollie got some more drinks in. She hadn't seen Chris so happy since he had fallen off Pixie. He grabbed his pint, swigged, and looked Mollie in the eye. He shouted in a drunken slur and the others just listened.

'Do you know what this lot said to me?... I've spent all my life here. And it's only now, NOW they tell me they've always known that while I was in the same team, I wasn't wearing quite the same uniform? Those bastards knew what I didn't all this time and they NEVER SAID A THING. I never knew I had such great mates, and you and Sandy and Gary...' His voice mumbled, and suddenly with a big grin on his face, he passed out.

The others looked at each other. 'How did that all come out?' Mollie demanded.

'It all started when he wanted to sing, and someone called him a big girls' blouse. He squared up to this bloke who apparently he went to Scouts with, who then told him to get it over and come out so they could do the gay jokes to his face! He'd had so much to drink, he just laughed and shouted 'I'm out but not quite as you'd like to think!' For some reason that got such a big laugh, they switched the karaoke on for him and this is his third song. We thought we'd join in, too,' Sandy was now looking wobbly, too.

'Don't count me in on that one,' laughed Gary. 'I'm mainstream!' Another bout of drunken giggling broke out, and Mollie knew it was time to get them home. She was the only one sober, so she got them out to the truck through catcalls and various rude jokes, shouts and cheers and they piled in, Chris snoring solidly. Mollie thought of setting his alarm for milking, but she couldn't be that mean when he had been so happy. Maybe things were changing for the better, but she wouldn't want Chris's hangover.

TWENTY-ONE

Mollie was right on that one. Chris woke the next morning wondering who had assaulted him this time, but then it all came rolling back. They had known all along he was not the same, said nothing and that was a gleam of joy in the darkness. But then again, the thought came; they thought he was gay, not a freak. The blackness swamped him again with the fury of the morning after. Nothing had changed, except that maybe the odd glass of beer might help him when it was at its worst. He opened one eye and saw the pills and pint glass of water by the bed. Mollie, bless her. He sat up and saw the morning was nearly gone, but he needed to bring some bales down for the cows. He groaned and dressed slowly.

The music was on in the kitchen, but not too loud, so why did Mollie have to shout if he wanted breakfast? The thought of food made him feel green. He sat with his head in his hands. 'Did I make a complete fool of myself last night?'

'No, I think you renewed some old friendships and they were so happy to have you back with them. Sandy pulled as well, or so he thought last night and Gary was just embarrassed by it!'

Chris managed a grin at that. The dogs started barking in the yard at what seemed to be hooves. Mollie and Chris looked at each other. Not another broken fence? They donned wellies and went out to see, shutting the annoyed dogs in the house. There was now whinnying coming from the mares, who were galloping down the hill. So, it wasn't them. Around the corner they found the source; it was Keith. His crying wasn't of a joyous master; it was a cry of pain. He was wearing a head collar with a broken lunge line attached to it. Chris felt a pang of nausea, for Keith was covered in blood. The mares reached him and he began a low, sad knicker. They sniffed him through the fence and bolted away. He then began to rear in distress, but he seemed to be losing energy as his jumps got lower and lower until he stood with his head to the ground, blowing hard, his sides heaving and breaking out in a sweat.

Chris made the first move towards him, talking gibberish. Keith raised his head and made to move away but seemed tied to the spot. Carefully, Chris got closer and picked up the rope. Keith shied away, then stopped to the line and voice.

'What's happened to you, you silly blonde beast? Come here, old man, let me help.' Keith stood and huffed at Chris, as he looked at the wounds. Mollie was already on the phone to the vet as she walked across the yard to the loose boxes.

'Come on, boy, let's get you inside.' Chris pulled gently on the line, but the pressure sent Keith into a rear of panic. Chris let him calm and settle again. This time he unclipped the lunge and just took a gentle hold on the head collar. Keith was okay with this, but suddenly walking was difficult. Each step needed a pause. It was as if he was lame in each leg. The blood was slowing down a bit, but one wound on his belly was really dripping. Slowly, they made their way to the box. Mollie, in this time, had swept it clear, ready for the vet, but put down some water. Keith's shoes clanked as he came in and he jumped again. He calmed and Mollie shut the door. Mollie and Chris talked in whispers.

'Emergency box in the tack room. Hopefully it's still in date. Hot water. I'll keep him quiet.' Chris kept up the singsong voice and Keith's ears seemed to be following him as he looked at the wounds. The cuts seemed familiar. They were barbed wire tears and were all over him. Chris could only imagine that Keith had bolted and had jumped wire to fall on it. Maybe the line had caught, bringing him down. What could have scared him so much? Mollie seemed to be taking forever, but she returned just as the vet's car swung in. Without a word, he followed her into the stable carrying his treatment box. Keith was now shaking.

'What a state.' The vet shook his head. 'Let's reduce the pain; then we can have a look at him.' He loaded a syringe. They all turned as another car drove into the yard with a splash of mud on the wall. Keith jumped and stood, pressing himself to the wall. Outside, they could hear shouts.

'It's Tina from the yard. I'll get her out the way if you don't need me?' The men, trying to calm the terrified horse, just nodded. Mollie found Tina still shouting by the car.

'It's okay, he's in the stable. The vet and Chris are with him. You're not helping by shouting.' Mollie raised her voice to get Tina's attention, as she seemed to be hysterical. 'We'll go in and get them a coffee.' She slipped her hand through Tina's arm and dragged her into the house. She didn't bother to call the dogs off and forcibly sat her down at the table. Tina had gone quiet, and then began to snuffle and finally burst into tears. She let her go on for a while, then pushed a box of tissues across the table to her. She finally dried up and sipped the coffee.

'So just what happened, then?' At this, Tina began to sniffle again.

'Oh, get on with it; you haven't even seen how he is yet, so just tell us all.' She really was trying to be kind, but it was hard. Finally, after a big gulp, Tina got going. 'After Brownie died, we didn't have any horses we could turn him out with. He kicked the geldings to bits and the mares fought back. Liz was turning him either out in the round pen to let off steam or in the big field when it was empty, as the fence is great.'

'When did Brownie die?'

'About six weeks ago. We found her just laid out in the paddock.'

'Well, she was in her thirties.'

Mollie gulped. 'But did that work, despite losing Brownie?'

'Only until one of the mares came in season and he jumped into the yard just as a ride was going out. Then Liz said he would have to be lunged or free schooled in the indoor school when there was no one about and it worked for a while. Then when Liz left, we had to cope with him.'

'Where's Liz then?' Asked Mollie in surprise.

'She had another huge argument with Diane and she sacked her.'

'How long ago was that?'

Tina's lip wobbled. 'About a month. Ann is coming back from Austria to take over, but there's been a holdup and she won't arrive for a few weeks. I've been running the place in the meantime.'

'What happened today?

'Well, we had a quiet day, so we thought we'd put him in the school to let off steam. He'd been yelling all morning. We put the head collar and lunge line on to get him across the yard. The others were hanging on the other side, but once he got through the door he reared up, threw us all to the side, and took off. He cut my hands really badly.' Mollie forbore to ask why Tina hadn't got gloves on. 'He went straight for that barbed wire fence at the end of the lane; we couldn't keep up with him. He jumped it clear, but the line caught in it and pulled him down as he landed. He caught his side and legs. We were all running like crazy. But he got up and pulled until the line broke and he took off. The same happened at the other end of the lane. He fell, but got up and galloped. We decided to split up. Sue went to ring the police and Heather went to get her car and go round the far side of the woods and I came up this way in mine. But he'd disappeared; then I thought of here...' Her voice trailed away.

'You really are unbelievable, Tina. Exploded Mollie. 'For someone who claimed to be better qualified than me, who knew it all, you broke all the basic rules of horsemanship. Gloves, bridle, surcingle, side lines, boots, helmet, calming supplements, calling Stan, are just a few of the words I'm thinking. Your poor management has ruined a very valuable horse. '

Tina wobbled again, but Mollie was right out of sympathy. 'If you can keep quiet, we will go and see. No squeaking-right?' She nodded and followed Mollie tamely to the stables. They peered carefully over the door, Mollie with a warning hand on Tina's arm. Inside, Keith was standing with his head to the floor, his legs braced as the vet and Chris worked. Mollie allowed her one gasp before she pinched her. Some cuts on his body had been shaved and sewn up, making him look a bit like a quilt. They were now working on the cuts on the back legs and bandaging them up. One of his knees was bandaged too. He had a rug over his quarters and the shivering and sweating seemed to have stopped. Then the two went to look under Keith's stomach.

'If this cut had been half a centimetre deeper, he would have been dead with his guts hanging out. This is the thinnest skin on the body. He really should be sedated in the hospital, but I don't want to move him. I will put a bandage right around his body to hold the stitches in place. I can't see any other way, and it would be good if he could be kept standing tonight, as cruel as that seems. Someone's head is going to roll for this.' Tina backed away at that. 'I think I should call the others and let them know, don't you think?' she whispered.

'I think you might need to talk to the police.'

A patrol car arrived in the yard. Tina gave a scream, but Mollie held her as she tried to get away. She motioned to the policeman to be quiet and shoved Tina. 'Man up and get this sorted; you owe it to Keith.' Tina gave her a filthy look but went to talk to the officer. Shortly afterwards, he left with Tina following in her car. Mollie heaved a sigh of relief and picked up her phone to ring Joanna, who would have to break all this to Diane. She couldn't see Tina doing it.

The vet had done all he could and was packing his things up.

'Could you two do with something to eat and drink? It's getting dark.' They nodded, and she sped off and, on her return, found them banking up a deep bed of straw in case Keith did fall.

'Do you know who insures him?'

'When I worked there, we weren't privy to all that, but I imagine it's all in the office. Tina will have to sort that in the morning.'

'When I was driving up, it was on the local news that he galloped up the main street of Hazeley, blood and gore everywhere.'

'He certainly took an odd route.'

'Right, I must go.' He handed the cup back. 'I have all the photos. I'll write the report as soon as I can, and I'll be back in the morning, but you can call me anytime.'

Mollie was taken back to a similar situation not a few weeks ago.

'Are you okay, Chris?'

'I'm fine, except for that hangover headache. Could you get me some more pills? Oh, and find a sleeping bag for me; I'll stay with him.'

Headache or not, he seemed to be the old Chris

again, and that had to be something positive. The cows were starting to shout about their full udders, so Mollie got Chris all he needed and went to milk. Much as she liked the cows, she really was getting tired of the constant pull on her life, it made her feel tied. Gary seemed to have the right idea with beef cows, no five a.m. starts there.

Chris sat on the straw and watched. Keith was well and truly out of it. He would wake in the morning and wonder what the party had been like; it must have been a good one. Did he feel each wound, each torn tendon? Would he wake in the morning and try to get up and shout for the mares, only to find his body not working and hurting? Would Keith even see the long-term and find life not worth living? Would he be wanting to be back to work as a stud and go in as if nothing had happened in his pea-sized brain. Whatever, Chris could feel the suffering, and it was a sudden balm not to be alone in a place of pain.

Later that night, with a thermos flask and a pack of sandwiches, Chris laid the sleeping bag as close to Keith as was safe and lay down. He dozed off quickly but was woken by something tickling his face. He opened his eyes to see a dopey looking Keith an inch from his face. He reached up and stroked the sleepy face. He huffed gently and closed his eyes, and so the two slept on and off until sunrise. Then Chris got up and checked the wounds for bleeding. All seemed holding. Keith was still sleepy, but his eyes were wide open, Chris could read the world of pain through the dope. At least he could help. He gave the patient another dose of painkillers. The two rested together in the early morning light. It seemed that together, they were at peace.

The next few days were critical. Keith ran a temperature and had to have intravenous antibiotics, and Chris only left his side to wash and eat. But Keith was allowed loose in the box at night to lie down. Chris often found he was sleeping against a warm back or a snuffly hairy face. But being a horse, Keith was soon looking for feed, hay and water. And for that, he had to move. He didn't seem to have a hangover from the sedative, but the milder ones kept him from wanting to do much more.

To Chris's surprise, Keith would knicker when he returned from his brief trips away and began to watch his every move. In treating the wounds, Chris felt that in some way he was treating himself. The reverse of his own healing; he was returning something. He couldn't quite get his head around it. Keith didn't react with anger as dressings were changed and some stitches had to be re-sewn; he was a shadow of his earlier imperious self. The binding around his belly was replaced with a big dressing and things looked better.

They could move Keith now, and one sunny morning they took him out onto the yard. They didn't think he would be stupid and try to get away, but put straw down to stop him slipping. He stood at the stable door looking out, scared to go over the threshold, shaking. It was clear that each stride was stiff and sore, but with each one, he loosened up a bit. Chris took each painful step with him, his body echoing the pain he had felt, too. Together, they made progress.

Keith's appetite returned fully and after two weeks, Chris decided he could return to his own bed, even though the vet had said Chris didn't need to stay with Keith after a few days. He shut the stable door, a little worried, but Mollie checked Keith later that evening and he was dozing. It was as if the companionship was more important to the two of them, a bond. Chris knew he was ignoring the work of the farm, but the kinship he felt with his wounded friend was healing him, too.

As Chris lay in the blissful softness and warmth of a mammoth soak in the bath, he realised that he hadn't thought about himself the whole time and something was lifting in him at last. It was as if the advent of Keith had put things into perspective. The way Keith reacted to him and looked to him was a balm to his soul; he wasn't alone. The trouble was, how would things go when Keith got better and was moved back to the yard?

TWENTY-TWO

Mollie and Tina were watching Chris on the yard. He had a bucket of water and was slowly washing away the last of the blood stains. Keith wasn't tied, but stood there picking his way through some hay like any old kids' pony. He moved over at a word from Chris and only swung his head gently if Chris touched something sore. The late winter sunshine had a bit of warmth in it, and the world was good.

'What did Diane say?'

'It was good she's 1000 miles away; as it was, I had to hold the phone away from my head. I let her rant, then apologised again and again. It seemed to work. I took responsibility for it all. I guess it helped when the insurance guys accepted the claim. I can't thank you enough for helping me sort that office out.'

'No problem. I couldn't believe what a mess she had left things in; it was always control, control, control. The accountant says there's money missing, too. I'm glad I didn't have anything to do with it all. How are the girls doing?'

'It's easier without Keith, I must admit. Diane's talking about moving him to a stud in Wales, but with those scars, who will look past him to use him?'

'Don't forget, he's the last of the line. His bloodline is really very valuable. I don't think it'll be a problem. What will you do when Ann arrives?'

'I think it's time to make a clean break. I do need to finish my training. I can go to Hartly for a year; then I'll see. And I am so sorry for being such a bitch.'

'One apology was enough, Tina. I really didn't know you had worked at the yard in the past. I can also see how Liz lied to you, and all the misunderstandings we built up, along with your home life. Water under the bridge and all that... Now, who's that coming? There seems a permanent trickle of people in and out of here these days. Oh, it's Chris's uncle and aunt. Look, excuse me. I'd like to say hello to them. Call me if you have any more problems?'

Tina nodded and went. Mollie was going to go over, but something stopped her. There was hugging going on; maybe now wasn't the time. She could go and wash up and then take some tea over.

Chris was as surprised as Mollie at his visitors. He was hugged by them both, which was unusual, but he soon found out the reason.

'Henry heard down at the pub that there's been a big accident with a horse on your farm and there had been injuries. We had to come and see if you are okay, and it seems like it was pub gossip, after all. It was only the horse!'

'Yes, he was scared and bolted and fell on barbed wire. He's healing well. Let me put him back in the box and we'll go in. Now you're here there's something I really need to ask you.' Their arrival had made him realise that he had someone to ask about the past after all. Keith followed him back into the box, and once rugged up, began to stuff his face. In the kitchen, Mollie took the hint and went to do something with the cows; she knew there was something private afoot.

'You finally want to know about your childhood?'

Chris took a mental step back. 'You have been waiting for me to ask?'

'Well, after your parents' accident we expected a lot to come out of the woodwork, but it didn't. We thought you were about to on your birthday. Why the sudden interest?'

'We found my mother's diary and a load of court reports. I never knew I had a problem.'

'You don't, Chris. It was only doctors wanting to use you as a guinea pig for their cracked ideas. We all discussed it together. You're a boy, you grew up a boy, but you are free to decide. Your parents and I did all we could to protect you from the media. You were child X; we had court orders, reporting orders, you name it. It seemed to work. But it was Rev Jones who sealed it. Have you read the transcript?

'No, that one I haven't seen.'

'We may have a copy. We'll get it to you. You need to read it, but just to say; he told the court what the effect the operations, and the treatments had been on his life due to the same condition. The jury was so shocked that the case was thrown out and the social services ordered to desist. They had witch hunts of their own to follow in those days. Taking kids away from their parents was high fashion in the 80s. '

All leaned back or took sips of tea.

'And you decided to keep me completely ignorant?'

'We agreed that we would tackle your questions as they came, and you never seemed to be concerned.'

'The home schooling?'

'Simple, swimming was coming up and we felt it would leave you open to bullying and other stuff.'

It all made sense. But Chris was nevertheless gobsmacked.

'You know all my mates think I'm gay?'

'That's the lesser of all the evils these days; let them go on thinking that.'

It was both a relief and more confusing to Chris. 'When did Rev Jones die?'

'He's not dead! He lives in a community in Dorset. He didn't come to the funeral of your parents because he was poorly. He sends us a Christmas card each year.'

If only he had been there, things would have been so much easier and maybe wouldn't have happened. Chris felt a whole new burden falling upon him.

'When your parents were in court, we used to

look after you. You made up for our own lack of children. You were such a sweet kid.'

Chris cringed; he couldn't remember any of this. 'Sorry, I don't remember, except you are my very special uncle and aunt.'

'Well, it was all over before you were three.'

'How can I thank you?'

'You don't need to. Family is family. But let all this sink in and then come for tea in a couple of weeks, and we can chat some more. We can see what paperwork we have. We all loved you, Chris. It doesn't matter what you may be, you're you and that's enough.'

Chris was overwhelmed and glad when they soon made their goodbyes. He made his way to Keith without thinking. For the first time, Keith jumped when Chris opened the door. But he huffed and then let Chris hug him on his neck where he wasn't so hurt. Chris felt the pain leave him, but there was so much going on in his head. Regret. Frustration. He knew one thing; he had to find Rev Jones and talk to him. He buried his head in the smelly mane and tried to fight the blackness that was threatening to engulf him again.

'I thought I might find you in here!' Now he was really trapped, there was no escape.

'Hi, Chloe. I thought you might be around sometime.'

'Yup, I've got you by the short and curlies! God told me today was the day to talk to you.' She saw him wince. 'Now tell me the whole story.' So he did.

At the end of it, she took a breath and came into the stable.

'You, poor, poor child.'

'Don't call me that! I'm a freak and nothing else!' The anger and fury in his voice had Keith jumping away and nearly knocking Chloe over. He calmed Keith and returned to her.

'I'm an unnatural freak. I'm not gay, I'm nothing. They might have done better to kill me.' He continued, trying to keep the fury out of his voice. He stroked Keith as much for his own good, for there was a peace in the touch.

'I was living in a quiet, calm place. I could have lived my life like that. Ignorance was bliss. I could be the farmer with a few mates and have lived my life out on the land. Nothing unusual. Now I cannot even decide what to be and what to do. What little I have is damaged. They all think I'm gay. I was ruined before I started. I can't even decide whether I want a family or not, there's no point even in deciding.... Why was I made like this?'

'But you have lived all of your life like this, whether you were conscious of it or not. Why do you need to change things? Go on being you. Have you been to a doctor or the hospital to check just what condition you have? Things change so rapidly; there may be every hope for you. Then maybe you can decide to live the quiet life of the farmer, or you may marry, or you may just need a man to love, or no one at all.'

'What, and let them bundle me away and force treatment on me? Put me to shrinks. Who will brainwash me in this political correctness?

'There are private clinics and even Christian ones; you can go to one or more and make your own mind up.'

'So why did He let me be beaten up?' Chris shied away.

'We live in a fallen world. And you know, it's said some men are born like this, some are made it's the bit in Matthew 19. God didn't do this to you. He's been with you all along. It's not a case of letting. We are in this world and although the supernatural and God are ever with us, this is physical with supernatural forces acting on people. Did you pray about this?'

'What good would that do?'

'You could tell Him exactly how you feel. You're not the only one to be betrayed and beaten up. It's not what you are, but who you are that matters to Him, nothing else.'

Chris didn't reply for a moment, as something had come to his mind, forgotten in the blackness that had been around him. He had to be honest. 'There was one odd thing when I was driving back. I was sure there was someone in the truck with me. He was right at my side until I passed out in the barn. Oh my…' Chris sank to his knees. 'He was there all along?'

Chloe came over to Chris and took his hands. 'I'm praying for you now.'

Chris hung on to Keith as she prayed in words and in tongues. He felt the peace returning that had gone when his parents died. He knew that there was a man who had been beaten until he wasn't recognisable as a human being, and God loved him, not for what he was labelled as, but for who he was, one of the beloved. He began to sob, and Keith nuzzled and pushed him.

'Sorry, mate', he apologised to the horse and Chloe laughed. 'Do you feel a little better now you can turn back to safety?'

'Yes, I feel like I can fight that blackness.

'Tell me how Mollie came to be here. She was never your partner, was she?' Chris mocked her with his eyes at the dumb question and they both giggled. The two of them sat in the thick straw with Keith munching away rhythmically, and began putting the pieces of Chris's life into some order.

James was packing up his car, ready to return to London. He had had enough of country life, so the new work and possibly the new bird made him want to get back into the swing of things. His contract meant he needed to work and where better than in his flat in Chelsea? He had worked on the new bird with texts and things. He was sure he could swing things, and he'd soon have a housekeeper with services included. He needed to get in touch with his dealer anyway.

He was just rummaging on the dashboard when he came across a pair of earrings that must belong to Mollie. He wasn't going to have her whining for their return. He'd pop them in the post box on his way out. Driving to the farm, he saw there wasn't a post box. So he found some paper and rolled the earrings up. She'd find them if he left them by the door. He had no desire to meet her again; she had been an idle whim and a waste of time.

He gingerly crossed the mud and made his way up the path. There was a handy flower pot, and he left the bundle where someone was sure to see. Time now to scarper. He turned and nearly bumped into a middle-aged blonde woman who was following him up the path.

'Hi, I'm Chloe, can I help?'

He looked down into her blue eyes. His world shook and crumpled. She saw through into his soul in the couple of nanoseconds that she held his gaze. He suddenly became aware of his dirty and nasty soul. His deceitfulness and abuse of people. He was suddenly stripped of it all. There was something else, too. This woman was his nemesis; she was the lover that he had been looking for all his life. She was going to change everything. His nasty shallow world was cracked into pieces because he was going to love her until the end of his days. She now looked shaken, too. She had offered her hand and he had taken it without seeing.

'My name's Chloe,' she repeated in a soft voice. 'I

think we have met somewhere, somehow before…

Mollie found herself at a bit of a loss and decided to take herself for a walk and maybe pop in on Joanna. They must have sorted out Chris's mystery by now. The dogs were pleased to have some attention. In the past weeks, with all that had had been going on, they had been neglected.

The December air was bracing; soon it would be time to think of mince pies and Christmas cake. It would be nice with Sandy and Gary. Maybe they would join her and Chris for the day; both were a bit alone. She liked Gary. He never got cross with her if she messed up driving the tractor, which Chris did sometimes, and they shared a similar sense of humour. She liked his large, well-covered strength, but she couldn't work out if Sandy's crush on him was returned.

Joanna's dogs were in the garden at The Manor, so she let her gang into the garden so they could play. As usual, the front door wasn't locked, so she barged in. The house was quiet, but the cars were outside. She finally heard voices from upstairs.

'Hi, Joanna! Are you free?'

In response, Guy came to the top of the stairs with an enormous grin on his face and he beckoned her to come up. In the bedroom at the top of the stairs came the cry of a baby. Mollie rushed the last few steps. In the bed sat a glowing Joanna, cuddling a bundle of child.

'She's arrived a bit early. The midwife has just gone and we can't reach Chloe, so you're the first to meet her. Mollie, please meet Amber Sarah!' The bundle was thrust into Mollie's arms and she gazed into blue eyes that saw all and knew nothing. A little hand was waving out of the swaddling and it grasped hers. In that second, Mollie knew that her mother had got it all wrong. There was nothing more simple or beautiful as the wonder of a new baby, the miracle of motherhood. The cows had been showing her the simplicity and joy of it, and it was so right. Joanna was beaming at her.

'She's perfect! I'm so blessed!'

Guy returned with champagne. 'We'll save a glass for Chloe, and Amber will have to have two godmothers!' Together they toasted the baby, and their worlds in different ways were complete.

EPILOGUE

Spring had come early to Hazeley, and all was still good in the world. Green was everywhere and Mollie sat on the doorstep of the farmhouse, cup in hand, with the dogs at her feet. It was so good to take in the fresh air after the damp and cold of winter. From the fields behind her she could hear one of the not- so -small calves having a moo. Another minor dispute, probably about a patch of grass, or someone had been caught trying to take swift suck on a cow not their mother. The herd was slowly going over to sucklers; Chris was keeping the calves until they were weaned. That made Mollie feel good to see their happiness and peace in the field. Patience and Katharina had been sold to Andy to boost his own herd, but the calves were to come to the farm to be fostered. It made Mollie feel content, and the happiness of the cows seemed right. There was also the joy in only milking once a day or as needed; she could stroll down at a luxurious eight o'clock. Playing with her goddaughter was also a joy, especially as Amber was an early waker, so Mollie would take her out for fun, giving Joanna a break.

Chris came and sat beside her, plonking a bag on the ground. She looked at him in the light and saw how his face had filled out, and he looked at peace. She had watched the healing journey between Chris and Keith as the two became more mobile and got more into the world, each a bit stiff physically and mentally. But as they healed, they grew apart, but not in the bond. Chris had only to whistle and Keith would appear from nowhere on the hill, and Keith would often suddenly appear by the yard, as if he knew Chris was worried about something. All this made her think of life, God, and things spiritual, but she hadn't reached any conclusion except there had to be more than the legalism of the Catholic church.

'Are you all packed?'

'As much as I can put in one backpack. When do they arrive?'

'Well, Sister Jo said the minibus has to do the station run; then they will come up to us.'

'Are you really, really sure you want to go through with this?'

'Never more so in my life. If I can make a difference to one lost girl by her staying here, then I will be happy. Four will be enough to start with, then maybe we can extend into kids from the inner city...'Chris saw her eyes go dreamy again. They had spent a lot of time in the winter thrashing the plan out and then the electricians and plumbers had been in, putting in internet and new bathrooms. Decorating and fitting the house out had been Mollie's joy with his assistance. Now he was free to travel to Dorset. It had come as a huge surprise to find the Reverend lived in a small community less than an hours' drive away. But the two had kept the barriers up as if the past was a wall. They had skirted about the meeting quickly, waiting to talk and pray face to face, as emails had flown back and forwards, a neutral territory making it easier to say the words. Chris would stay there for as long as he needed. He was free. Mollie's money was subsidising him as far and wide as he wanted while she used his farm. They smiled at each other.

'No more compromise living for us anymore!'

'But some of it was fun!'

'But not forever.'

'I know. Yet we have something between us that's more than that, isn't it, Chris?'

He looked her in the eyes. 'Friends and buddies for life.'

They could hear a vehicle coming up the lane, so he turned to her and for the first time they touched and hugged each other in complete sympathy. Then from the hill came the imperious call of a stallion.

'Oh, no, he thinks it's mares arriving.' Down the hill came a scrappy, moth- eaten looking palomino stallion, who was still a bit lame, but the gleam was back in his eye and he was ready for the spring. He yelled again, then took back off up the hill as a very round, pregnant Dixie was neighing to call him back.

'He certainly hasn't changed much, has he?'

'Not a jot! But it's just as well he doesn't have a mirror. He thinks he's totally back to normal. Are you sure you can cope?'

'Gary is around if I need him.' Mollie was blushing furiously. Sandy had fallen in love with another plumber in Southampton and wasn't around and in that time, much had changed.

'I really must go! Come on, Rex, into the chariot!'

Chris held Mollie's hand, then with a shrug, turned and as he did, Mollie smiled with a love from deep in her heart that set him free to be whoever he wanted to be.

DEAR READER,
THANK YOU!

I do hope you enjoyed Mollie's and Chris's adventures, they continue in Chaos, an excerpt follows.

Please leave a review on Amazon or stars on Goodreads. It means so much to indie authors!

There are many ways to catch up with my books. My blog, Anna's Horse Books, acts like a mailing list. Once a month will come books, interviews, special offers, and much more. There is also an Advent Calendar which will give you loads of ideas for Christmas horse book gifts! On the Homepage, just click on follow by email at the foot of the page, or click on the follow widget if you are on Wordpress.
https://booksbyanna619772285.wordpress.com/

You can also join me in my Facebook group for horse book readers! Horse Books for Grown Ups

https://www.facebook.com/groups/1979909005465261

You can find my Author page on Facebook

https://www.facebook.com/horsesandogs

Twitter: Anna Rashbrook@AnnaRashbrook

Now, please turn the page for a little taste of Chaos!

CHAOS

MOLLIE

Mollie sat with her head in her hands on the sofa. Why had she ever thought she could do this? Why had she never considered what it might be like from the other side? She thought she knew teenagers, what it would be like, but this was nothing like she expected. She tried to run through the day's events to see where she had gone wrong. Sister Jo had been adamant that she would not stay and see them settle in and had taken off in a cloud of dust in the minibus, perhaps Mollie should have read the warning signs then.

The four girls stood there, looking dumbfounded and embarrassed, stuffed backpacks. The youngest thawed out first, Sarah as Mollie remembered from the notes they had sent her. Twelve. Just on the cusp of it all. The other three were fifth formers and from their body posture they didn't want to be here, or maybe anywhere at all.

'Right, I'm Mollie, as you know, so come on in and fight over the bedrooms!' She led the way hoping they would follow, and like quiet little sheep they did. She could almost sense the hostility as they thumped up the stairs.

'Now, you have a room each, look and then decide.' They shuffled and looked in each door, Sarah always being the last and getting pushed to the back. Should she make an issue and make the others let her see in first?

'I'll take this one,' stated the blonde one, and to her surprise, Sarah butted in, I want one that looks over the stables.'

'That's the last one then. What about you other two?' They just took one of the door handles and went to go it. 'Now hang on a minute! The password is written on the board on the back of the door. All of you have en-suite showers I'm afraid because the water comes from the hill and the pressure isn't high, but it heats on demand so you can take long showers. The water here is hard. You will need more stuff than normal. There are extra blankets and pillows in the cupboards. If you want to put up pictures, please not on the exterior walls, they're hard and nothing sticks. Settle in and food is in half an hour.'

The silence was deafening, not golden and Mollie slunk her way downstairs, her heart in her boots. In the kitchen she put the bacon on to fry, double checking her list that there were no dietary problems and laid the table. It was also a relief that none wanted to go to Mass, either. She could hear the footsteps on the floors above and wondered what they were all thinking. It took her back to the first time she was dumped on someone, although only ten, she had felt so awkward, didn't know what to do or say, what she could touch or do, no one gave her any clues, it was just expected that she would understand when mealtimes were and where to leave her boots. OMG, had they brought wellies? She looked out of the window and to her relief saw a line of them abandoned on the yard.

'Um, where do I leave my riding kit?' It was Debbie, the blonde and most scary one.

'Just through that door, there are hooks and stuff.' Mollie had forgotten the dogs, and the door opened to a cacophony of noise from Mutantmutt and Ratty, oh, no she would get mobbed. She waited for the shriek. It didn't come.

'Oh, babies, you're so cute!' It was a squeal of joy. Debbie was on the floor getting washed and wagged at with huge enthusiasm. 'What's their names?' Mollie spent a happy couple of minutes telling Debbie all about the dogs then they all came back into the kitchen where the dogs found three more members to their fan club. Eventually, the fun wore off, and the girls looked at Mollie for what's next, which turned out to be burning bacon and clouds of smoke.

'What do I do, chuck it and start again?'

'Chuck it, we're vegan!' Grimaced Jenny with the red hair tied back from her face.

'You're what?'

'Yeah, we're doing it for Lent. Didn't Sister Jo tell you?'

CHRIS

There was a thundering on the door and Alan woke him, yelling up the stairs.

'Chris, we've got a problem. Can you come down?'

Rex went rushing out and Chris in milking mode threw his clothes on. Alan and Sam were hovering in the doorway, Alan with a piece of paper in his hands, which he thrust to Chris without a word.

Dear All,

It's time for me to move on. I have found a new job and somewhere to live. I've just been waiting on Chris's arrival and now he can take over the stables for me. I've written a list and messaged Kathy to tell her, so all is ready for this week.

Thanks so much for your love and healing, and I feel a new person. My identity in Christ is secure and I know I won't backslide. I will treasure my memories of you all, and maybe I'll pop back soon and we can catch up.

June

Chris felt like he was dowsed in a shower of iced water. He sat down without a word, only aware of a huge overwhelming rage he had never experienced before rising in him.

'No.' As he spoke, the anger came out. 'I will not do this. It's not what I came here for and you all know that. I've had enough of being tied to flaming animals and this is my chance to break away and begin afresh. I AM NOT GOING TO DO IT! Were you all part of the plan too? Find a mug to come along and dupe into working here?' His voice finished on a shriek. Alan laid a placating arm on him, but Chris shook it away.

'Get off me, don't you dare touch me!' Where was all that coming from flitted through his mind?

Chris, calm down!' Sam now intervened as a speechless Alan backed off. Her voice was suddenly deeper and stronger than before and it stopped him in his tracks. 'We're not asking you to! We just need you to come with us to the yard this morning and help us get it sorted. Calm down. We are just as annoyed as you are. She's left the flat a tip...Oh, and please don't flip again, we think she might have taken your truck, the mini is still here.'

Chris took flight and ran up the cliff path, his rage fuelling his speed, but he was gasping as he reached the crest. He didn't need to go further, he could see that it was indeed gone, he sank to the ground, breathing heavily Rex came bounding up, thinking it some new game, and for a split second, Chris wanted to shove the slobbering beast into the sea. But he couldn't and in remorse hugged the bewildered dog to him, 'You stupid dog, can't you leave me alone for five flaming minutes?' His sanity was returning as his face was washed. He would now have to and apologize and he both didn't want to, still feeling angry with them, even though they weren't guilty, it all still felt like a trap and he was suffocating inside. Nevertheless, he made his way back down to where they were sitting on the bench waiting. They waited for him to speak.

'It's gone. How she knew you can start it under the dashboard I don't know, I never told her. It wasn't locked. It has about a week's MOT on it. It leaks oil and the battery is on its way out. Serves her right.'

Printed in Great Britain
by Amazon